Following His Lead

Lessons learned from a drug kingpin, hearts of the homeless and the slums of Reynosa

Tina Swann

Following His Lead: Lessons learned from a drug kingpin, hearts fo the homeless and the slums of Reynosa
Tina Swann

Chapters in this book were published earlier in *It's Not Odd, It's God: Stories of God's Hand in Everyday Life © 2108*
Cover and Interior Page design by True Potential, Inc.
Cover photographs of the author courtesy of Joseph De Sciose

ISBN: 9781948794404

Milestones International
an imprint of:
True Potential, Inc.
PO Box 904, Travelers Rest, SC 29690
www.truepotentialmedia.com

Printed in the United States of America.

Prayer of St. Theresa of Avila

Let nothing disturb you.

Let nothing frighten you.

All things pass away. God does not change.

Patience achieves everything. God alone suffices.

God has no body now on earth but yours.

No hands but yours, no feet but yours. Yours are the eyes through which the compassion of Christ looks out on the world.

Yours are the feet with which he is to go about doing good.

Yours are the hands with which he is to bless his people.

Amen.

Foreword

When Tina asked me to help edit and promote her book I enthusiastically accepted her request. I had gone back to college in 2009 and graduated with a B.S. in Business Administration/Marketing. I loved learning so much that I pursued a Masters Degree in Marketing and Sports Management, graduating in 2014. Little did I know God had a purpose for me to use my knowledge and skills to help Tina pursue her dream to write her book.

I first met Tina through a Facebook request in 2009. We never met, but I followed her page and articles she would post. I couldn't help think how connected to God she was and how spiritual her postings were.

In 2011 a horrific tornado roared through Tuscaloosa, Alabama. One of my best friend's son was caught in the middle of it. Terrified, he and his two roommates huddled together in their condominium bathroom tub as the wind howled outside. When the winds subsided, they ventured out and surveyed the damage. Every house across the street was leveled, debris scattered everywhere. I posted a Facebook message to Tina asking her to please pray for these young men as they moved forward after this traumatic event. She wholeheartedly accepted. God had saved them.

Through the years I continued to read her postings and was awed by how God would touch her heart and Tina would respond accordingly. It didn't matter what or where. God placed her in some extremely dangerous situations, like helping a drug kingpin find the Lord, helping families in Reynosa, Mexico build homes amongst drug cartels, having to stay in a guarded compound at night for safety. She assisted the homeless, visiting in and around their 'tent cities' fearless of any dangerous situations she would encounter.

When God called, she would drop everything and follow through on His calling.

During the last nine years, I also would face some tough times in my own life. I was so blessed to overcome an addiction to alcohol in 2003 and start to live life one day at a time. I had a lot to repair. Relationships with family and friends. It was hard because of all the damage I had caused, but Tina would post just the right spiritual message I needed to hear. Her words seemed like they were directed to me, even though I still didn't contact her or write to her.

I lost my mother to a stroke in 2016, and through Tina's postings, her messages comforted my soul as I grieved her death. She was helping me, and she didn't even know it!

In late 2018 I finally found the courage (through God) to walk away from a very toxic marriage. I was lost and scared of starting my life over at 66. The decision to leave had to be done, but my heart struggled to let go as I grieved the loss of my marriage. It is tough, which pain is worse, staying in a toxic relationship or live alone (which terrifies me).

I reached out to all my friends to let them know of my situation. Tina was one of those friends. For the first time ever we communicated on the phone. Her soothing words comforted my soul and she said that I would be okay, telling me to give it all to God, that He would place his loving arms around me.

I have stayed in touch with Tina ever since. I admire her dedication to the Lord, her unbelievable faith. I have never encountered anyone more spiritually connected as her. God truly nudges her and she responds, helping in ways He directs her.

So when Tina asked me to edit and promote this book, it was God who nudged me. Yes, it would be an honor to do it.

Daniel Lewis

Acknowledgements

I would like to thank my publisher, Steve Spillman, for having faith in me and *It's Not Odd, It Is God*. The direction he provided when I was lost in this project and for all the encouraging words when I was overwhelmed and ready to give up. Thank you for always being there and especially giving me the most precious gift, publishing my book.

Thank you to Joseph De Sciose, for your wonderful photographs.

To my friends that have prayed for me, allowed me to share my stories with them and the encouragement to see the big picture. I am so blessed: Pam McCue, Gwen Baugher, Kathy Norton, Roberta Ress, Donna Cotten, Amy Cotten, Mary Crowell and William Hutton.

Karin McAndrew has also prayed over me, allowed me to cry on her shoulder when I was overwhelmed and was witness to some of the stories. For this, I thank you and will always be grateful.

I wish my father, Richard (Buddy) McGee, were here to see this book. He taught me to follow my dreams and never give up. He was a great role model and a man with a huge heart for others. Thank you Daddy!

Preface

This book opens a door to the awakening of consciousness, Tina Swann teaches us that we are not puppets in the hands of chance. Life is not an accident governed by luck or coincidence. Everything happens for a reason. Sublimely, the writer shows us that life is a causal connection. After reading this book you will begin to see life from a different perspective, knowing that everything as inexplicable as it may be, has a meaning.

In this book, Tina explores the different manifestations of spirituality in life, she shows us the obstacles we have to overcome in order to conquer that spirituality we need so much, in the only possible way: through Contact with God and the power of the Holy Spirit, understanding that God has a purpose for each one of us "

"5070. This number represents the miles that separates me from Tina and this book represents the number of reasons God has for us. It was not a coincidence I met Tina, and it is not a coincidence that you are reading this book right now. At that point you will discover that there are not only coincidences but Divine casualties"

Sonia Lamique

Introduction

Following His Lead is written to inspire and share with you, how amazing God is. As you turn the pages, story after story, hopefully these will penetrate your heart with a connection and memory of your own. Reflecting in your life of an account that now you know to be a God-Incidence and not coincidence.

You will read about being broken and in a pit, faith, accidents that would lead to blessings, gifts from God, people coming into my life as well as being removed and prophecy. God knew all of this and it was not a coincidence.

How many times have we said or heard, 'what a coincidence'? Allow me to explain why happenings in our lives are orchestrated by God. Personally, I am so thankful He loves and cares for me enough to open and close doors where need be and that I may be in alignment with Him whether I understand or not, His plans for my life. His plans are far better than mine.

Being aligned with God is the thought of pleasing Him. When you fall out of that lane, the tendency is to allow rebellion/sin to rear its ugly head. God will guide you and you rely on Him, not others diagnosing your life. Does life get difficult at times and you wonder where He is? Sure. I have certainly had my share, but it isn't one minute you are a believer and the next you are not. These difficult and challenging times are seasons where we gain spiritual strength. Believe!

God is:

- Omnipresence – Being present everywhere
- Omnipotence – Having unlimited power
- Omniscience – Unlimited knowledge
- Immutability – Unchanging in His character
- Infinity – God is timeless

"Behold I am the Lord, the God of all flesh....is anything too difficult for Me?" Jeremiah 32:27 (KJV)

Amazing God's unlimited power, knowledge, is unchanging, everywhere and timeless. But, we believe everything is a coincidence.

"He is before all things and by Him all things consist." Colossians 1:17 (KJV)

God loves us that much to be involved in every aspect of our life. These are just a few scriptures that demonstrate God's love for us and His promises. If you have parents, siblings, a spouse, children or dating someone special you know how loving them feels. That is exactly how God feels about us. But God's love is more than just a feeling, it is an action.

God gives us peace, joy and comforts us when we are hurting and fearful.

God lives us so much that He gave us His son. ***"For God so loved the world that he gave his one and only son, that whoever believes in him shall not perish but have eternal life."*** John 3:16

Would you be willing to sacrifice someone you love? He did.

God shows mercy through Jesus Christ that died so that we may have life. Jesus gives us life, even when we are knee deep in sin. Jesus died in our place. It does not matter what you have done, God still loves you.

"For the eyes of the Lord run to and fro throughout the whole earth to show Himself strong in the behalf of them whose heart is perfect toward Him." 2 Chronicles 16:9

He is watching over all of us, but does allow free will. So the decisions you make play a part in circumstances and your future. God will never leave nor forsake you. You may be the one walking away.

"Let your conversation be without covetousness and be content with such things as ye have; for he hath said I will never leave thee nor forsake thee." Hebrews 13:5 (KJV)

His word clearly states He will never leave us and He establishes our steps as in Proverbs 16:9. If this is so, God is in control and everything that happens in your life is not by accident. I would say things happen as "God-Incidence."

Technically, a coincidence is an occurrence of events that happen at the same time by total accident.

"Look at the birds, they do not plant seeds, gather a harvest and put it in barns; yet your Father in heaven takes care of them! Aren't you worth much more than birds?" Matthew 6:26 (TEV)

Again, coincidence is not planned. But, Jeremiah 29:11 says ***"'For I know the plans I have for you' declares the Lord. 'plans to prosper you and not harm you, plans to give you hope and a future.'"***

Events that happen, even when they don't make sense, are blessings from God. He is involved in our lives, but sometimes we don't see His guiding hand, until we get knocked down.

Take every opportunity to grow with scripture and prayer, may you understand a life lived by God's principles. May this book renew hope, restore your heart and refresh faith that demonstrates God's presence in our lives. I invite you now to travel with me on this exciting journey.

You may not see the full view, but as you take your seat and allow God to pilot through, the scenery will become breathtaking. Then when you have come to the end, trace your steps and think about what led you to this book. God has plans for your life and maybe on this day, the plan and life clicked together.

Climb on board and rely on Him!

If you followed the life of Joey Feek, country and gospel singer, along with her husband Rory Feek. You know that she passed away March 4, 2016 from terminal cancer. After her passing Rory took her home to Pottsville, Tennessee for her final resting place.

My neighbors Sheryl Walker Putman, her husband Jim Putman and their son Bradley Walker are very dear friends of the Feek family. Bradley, also a singer, has taken stage with Joey and Rory at the Grand Ole Opry as well as their home in Tennessee. Joey and Rory were nominated in 2016 for a Grammy Award.

When Bradley played with them it was mostly country and bluegrass. Joey had said in an interview with People Magazine, before her passing, "But, I don't fear anything because I'm so close to God and we've talked about it so many times. I know he's close. And I know he loves me. I'm at peace."

Because of the strong bond between the families, Bradley was invited to sing at Joey's memorial service and asked to sing a particular hymn that was her favorite. After the service, the well known Bill Gaither, singer and songwriter of southern gospel and contemporary Christian music, asked who sang the song. The Feek family told him that it was Bradley Walker. This is how God orchestrates people in our lives. Bradley has been a singer for years and has never given up on following his dream to reach people and be heard. Bradley was placed at this service for a season and it was to be heard by Bill Gaither. The meeting of the two led to a video taping to be released in the fall. Not in country music, but now as a Christian artist. God is good, all the time.

CONTENTS

The Journey

I am so blessed to be given this opportunity of sharing *Following His Lead* with you. God entrusted me with His plan in touching lives from a drug Kingpin (a narcotrafficker/candy man) to the homeless, to a young high school athlete and all the way to Reynosa, Mexico.

It took me literally a year to see how God was using me because I didn't feel qualified. I am a nobody, God. They may not believe me, God. I am not gifted in eloquent writing, God. And many times it has been said: "Please don't ask me to do this, get someone else." (Proverbs 3:5-6)

Trusting Jesus isn't always easy. He was asking me to trust Him over the fear I felt of the unknown and unseen. These stories will take you through a walk of faith.

"But God doesn't call us to be comfortable. He calls us to trust Him so completely that we are unafraid to put ourselves in situations where we will be in trouble if He doesn't come through." Francis Chan

As I was reflecting on the journey of *Following His Lead*, I hear this message 'Overcoming Obstacles' by Dr. David Jeremiah. This was a God-incidence! He was showing me from the dream and birth of this book through setbacks, enemy attacks, betrayal and distractions that He was there carrying me through every step and paving the way.

Follow along as we look at the bumps, turns and twists on the road to Following His Lead. Even the best route isn't all sun-filled meadows and quiet creekside lanes. This journey experienced hard terrain and deep valleys. What got me through was following God who knew perfectly the right path. He had mapped out the way before me. He was fully aware of every obstacle and pit, and sidetrack that would tempt me.

After writing 'Blooming Out of the Ashes' for the Best Seller *Beyond the Woman*, I began entertaining the thought of writing my own book. But these thoughts were like a revolving door coming in, and I would push them out. I did this because writing was challenging for me.

However, God had other plans. In February 2016 I was in a crazy powerful dream when my alarm went off. The impression in my mind was so strong, it went straight to my soul. I knew this was a divine message because I had already been thinking of writing this book.

Most of these stories were already in place then a dear friend brought this to my attention. He said, "These stories are amazing Tina, but it is more about how God has used you to touch so many lives and in different ways." Honestly, I didn't see it that way because I had been so involved with each story. I thought of Christian leaders and speakers of being anointed, just not myself.

"Now all Christians are anointed, chosen for a specific purpose in furthering God's Kingdom." (1 John 2:20)

Taken from the song 'I Can See Clearly Now' by Johnny Nash.

"I can see clearly now the rain is gone, I can see all obstacles in my way. Gone are the dark clouds that had me blind. It's gonna be a bright, bright Sun-Shiny day."

Placing my thoughts to pen and paper, was a struggle. Many times I felt so lost searching for words to bring a story to life. My library of words was murky, to say the least. Yet the creativity was crystal clear. I was so frustrated I just wanted to put it away and maybe one day pick it back up. God knew I needed a little spark to get the "fire in my belly" and in His perfect timing, the words began to flow. So much so that I was writing every chance I had. When one story was coming to an end, God was providing details for the next. A beautiful collection.

God had placed this on my heart, and I was determined to see it through, so the enemy decided to entice me by distracting me with a beach trip. When you haven't had a vacation in three years, this was like winning the lottery. I struggled whether to accept the invitation and have a break from writing or stay home and continue with the manuscript. All expenses paid beach trip versus writing. Hmmmm....

After much thought and prayer, writing won. I had committed to reaching my publisher's deadline, and I needed to stay on point. Not only did I give up a trip, I also disappointed my friend. Writing *It's Not Odd, It's God* (this book's original title) wasn't always a popular decision. I had friends that turned against me. Despite the hurt, I had made the decision to believe in God's plan for these messages.

Colossians 3:15 says, "Let the peace of Christ be the controlling factor in your hearts."

After several months of writing, the manuscript was ready for release. The day I placed this in the mail my precious friend Anthony from 'Anthony's Story' in the book passed away. I was grateful that our story opened the book and even more so now; however, my heart was shattered into a million pieces. I felt blessed that I was becoming an author of a book, but it didn't seem to hold that special place any longer because my friend was gone. Nonetheless, it was on its way to the publisher and no turning back now. Even though my publisher had the manuscript and was reviewing each story, God was still at work. He was continuing to open doors and place people in my path. He even took me to Mexico so that I may share 'The Passport' with you, which was the last story before editing and binding the book for publication.

Steve Spillman, my publisher, had shared that my book would be released by the Christmas holidays of 2016, but for different reasons, this didn't happen. My hope all along was that it would be published in the spring. The book would bloom like flowers, a refreshing fragrance of God's word. And we know everything happens in God's perfect timing. Hold this thought and let me share this.

While I was anxiously awaiting the book publication, my mother became very ill and was hospitalized for a month before passing away. With the unexpected death came funeral arrangements and all the obligations that were required from this.

Not only was I physically and mentally exhausted, but I was also about to be blindsided by betrayal and a gut-wrenching evil. The day following the funeral I received news that my family inheritance was stolen by someone close to the family, but not blood kin. Not only was I trying to wrap my head around this intentional evil act, it was also thrown in my face that they had acquired it all. It was as though the granddaughters and I never existed. The bloodline wiped clean. To honor my father I wanted to make sure their property wouldn't be vandalized, so I went to check on it only to be met by law enforcement asking me to leave MY family's property. A house that my father worked so hard for and passed away in, and I was no longer welcome. Devastating is an understatement. But I chose to take the high road and walk away releasing this to God. Reminding myself that He is my avenger.

Do you remember me talking about my hopes for the book's release date?

After the death, betrayal, and evil at its finest---I was notified that my book was now available on Amazon and through Barnes and Noble. God's love and light were shining brightly. *It's Not Odd, It's God* would bloom out of brokenness.

What I learned also was marketing and promotion was just as challenging as the writing. The original book has been blessed with 5-star reviews through Amazon and has traveled to Australia, Japan, Canada, and India.

But God is not finished. He wanted me to continue with the second edition. He has whispered, "If you will take my hand, I will show you."

"Your word is a lamp to my feet and a light to my path." Psalm 119:105

God has a plan for each and every message in this book, and I have given this entirely to Him. May His will be done, not mine.

"For I am not ashamed of the gospel of Christ for it is the power of God to salvation for everyone who believes." Romans 1:16

He desires to see your purpose fulfilled and His plan come to fruition. And will walk beside you as a Guide and Comforter so that you never face the twists and turns of life alone.

Tina Swann

The Butterfly Feeling

People may think of a cocoon as a resting place, there's no resting going on inside the cocoon! To the contrary. Insects that spin cocoons must eventually escape from them to complete their transformation. The adult butterfly will break its casing before emerging."

That is how I feel. I feel like a million butterflies trying to break through. Many have heard the phrase, "I am going to jump out of my skin." Until I act on the prompting from God, this sensitive feeling will continue. Some may ask if I always have this feeling and the answer is no. Sometimes God has orchestrated a meeting with someone, and I feel the nudge upon meeting then later He leads me.

"For as many as are led by the Spirit of God, these are sons of God." Romans 8:14

Some may feel uncomfortable with this and choose not to go deeper with the Holy Spirit. Maybe God is using me in this way because I have given Him the green light to do so.

"The Spirit Himself bears witness with our Spirit that we are children of God." Romans 8:16

The Holy Spirit cannot help you with things unless He can communicate with you. When you begin to communicate with Him, you will learn by trial and error.

He may lead or prompt you. He may give you a feeling like it is a stop sign. You may hear a message and feel like it is directed specifically for you, it is knowledge you need to hear.

It is up to you whether or not you learn and experience the Holy Spirit in your life. If you want more of God, in a supernatural way, don't be afraid to tread in deep water with Him.

Anthony

The first Saturday of the month an Outside Church service is held for citizens of homelessness. Friends begin gathering around 10:30 with the service beginning at 11:00 followed by a wonderful buffet style meal. If you are not familiar with the homeless, many times they shy away from a crowd but only come by later to receive their meal. This is open to all, and a way to serve. We are called to feed the poor and help those in need. Isaiah 58:7 says, "Share your food with the hungry, and give shelter to the homeless. Give clothes to those who need them, and do not hide from relatives who need your help."

This particular April morning, as people gathered, I noticed a very large muscular, African American male standing across the creek, away from the others just observing. As I watched, no one was speaking to him, but he seemed to know many who were there. The Holy Spirit was leading me to walk over and meet him. As I moved closer to him, I noticed he was watching me and looked at his phone several times, seemed a little nervous. We did the formal introductions and he made comment that he was there for the meal and had never attended the service. God always has a plan! As our conversation began he told me that he wasn't homeless. He knew many people from the streets, but he was in town to care for a sister riddled by cancer. I stayed with him through the service and joined him for lunch. He asked me if I would come by sometime and pray with her and the family. My thought was, "Sure, not any time soon. I don't know you." Well, he gave me his number and said to text or call him when I felt comfortable. Me thinking, "Might be awhile."

Well God had different plans. The next day, Sunday, I guess God thought it was comfortable, because He nudged me to contact him and extend the invitation to join me in church. Everything in my flesh was fighting back in reference to contacting him, but I did. I called him and he was very gracious, but declined due to his sister's health.

When Monday evening came, I was leaving the gym, and again that nudge for me to call him. My flesh was pushing back, no not again, I don't even know him or his family. God, pick someone else to do this. Nope, not doing it.

Not audibly, but the Holy Spirit was persistent in reference to this call.

Finally, I picked up the phone and called. This is what he said, "Why did you call?"

I told him I was just checking on him to see how he and his sister were doing.

Here is the WOW of how God works. His response, "You couldn't have called at a better time. I can't see a light at the end of the tunnel. It is so dark and I am so low." We talked for an hour and I shared the Lord with him. He had never had anyone share the gospel with him.

We communicated several times during the week and he became more peaceful hearing about a walk with the Lord. Then he shared with me. "The day I met you I saw you walking towards me and thought....what does this white girl want? I told you every story I could think to scare you so that you would walk away but you didn't. Then normally my phone would ring several times. Not one time did it ring. I continued to look at my phone to see if it was even working."

I couldn't help but laugh listening to this because I knew God had me there for a reason. Then he said this, "No one has even shown an interest like this."

As I ministered to him we became friends. He shared his life with me. That he had been in prison for armed robbery. I asked if that were businesses or homes. He told me both, and that he had been known on the streets as the "Bad N***er". Should I be nervous? That was a past life and he was no longer involved with that or associated with his past. He had such a sensitive heart, that it was difficult to imagine a criminal background. That was just it, the past. It no longer existed, he was moving forward and away from the name he held for years. Sometimes, you need to move away from old habits to have a fresh start. We all make mistakes and thank the good Lord we are given many chances to take a negative and make it into a positive. This is exactly what my new friend was trying to do, yet a cloud of shame was pouring rain of guilt on him. God knew this and placed us together for a reason. We worked together on changing the way he was thinking, deleting his past and focusing on goals if the future. He was excited about the difference in his life and the ones that loved and cared about him were also seeing change. That meant a new life for him.

I met his family, prayed with his sisters and felt like I belonged. A year went by and he moved to another city, about two hours away. We stayed in touch and when he came home, we always got together. He kept me posted on his sister's condition and I would occasionally visit them.

I was working at the gym and one morning and received a message from him that his sister was dying and he couldn't get home in time. I asked what I could do to help. He said, "Will you please go see her and let her know I will be fine and not to worry about me." I left the gym arriving at there by 7:00. With several family members around her, I didn't feel comfortable asking if I could see her, but one sister whispered "Wait until the room clears and then go in and talk to her. She would want to know you are here." At this time she was in a coma and her breathing was very shallow.

Everyone left and I went in to speak with her. I took her hand and began talking to her. I kissed her cheek and told her what an honor it was to be a part of their family. Thanking her for welcoming me into their home and said "Anthony can't be here, but wants you to know that he us doing well and you don't have to worry about him." She opened her eyes and looked at me and I said, "I knew you could hear me. The Lord has you and I love you." Her eyes closed and I left the room. I told the family goodbye, called Anthony and let him know that I had been his voice so that he would have peace. I received a call five minutes later that she had passed away.

Anthony and I said we would always share this story. My sweet friend, Anthony, passed away April 2017.

"The heart of man plans his way, but the Lord established his steps." Proverbs 16:9 (ESV)

How Great is our God!

In Loving Memory. I sure miss you.

Blooming Out Of The Ashes

I am so grateful and consider it such a blessing to have the opportunity to share this book with you. I truly hope you enjoy the stories, that they touch your heart and have an impact to change a life.

I am a woman who has experienced much despair in my life. I have experienced total desperation and have been without hope. At one point, I had only $3.00 to my name, wondering what I was going to do, and how I was going to make it. How would I afford food, gas to put into my car to get to work, pay my bills, and stay afloat? I was also dealing with people telling me to take on several jobs. How was that feasible, I could not even afford gas to go apply for jobs and online applications were not an option, I did not have internet service. I felt like I was drifting on a raft at sea with no lifeline anywhere in sight. Yet God, Who never leaves us nor forsakes us, gave me hope. In my deepest despair and most desperate times, God invaded my heart with hope and His love.

God did indeed give me hope, but many times I still felt like a wilted flower. Something or someone who wilts is weak, tired and exhausted. I was all of those. I lost all energy, had no confidence, and effectiveness I once had was gone. I was completely fatigued and exhausted in every area of my life. Fear would grip my heart, often to the point of paralysis. Panic and anxiety often overwhelmed me. I was routinely bombarded with feelings of hopelessness. We all can easily come to a place where we just throw up our hands and say "What is the use?"

My walk was often hard, burdens were heavy, and my life seemed empty and unrewarding. However, I did everything I could to keep busy. I knew that idleness in my life would lend itself to me thinking too much. Whenever I gave in to idleness, I tended to have tremendous mood swings, or develop negative attitude, totally dependent on the circumstances in my life. My heart was broken, and I gave in to the natural tendency for my soul to drift into despair and negativity,

Right this moment you may be thinking, "I am broken and in despair right now myself. In fact, I often feel pretty worthless and not very useful to anyone at times." As I said earlier, I know exactly how you are feeling. I was overwhelmed by these thoughts throughout each day. But I did not quit. I did not give up. I encourage each one of you to decide today quitting is not an option. Decide for yourself right now that you are not going to give up on life. Also, make the decision that you are not going to give up on yourself. Know that there is a way out. There is hope for your life and any situation you may find yourself in right now.

You must begin to become very intentional concerning yourself and your life, your friends, and in everything you do. I intentionally made up my mind that I was going to bloom out of the ashes in my life. And I felt as thought I was living in an ash heap. My life and my environment had become very, very dark. However, I knew deep in my heart that God did not create me to let anxiety and fear permanently control me, or to live in despair and hopelessness the rest of my life. He created me to trust Him and have faith in Him. Each day I began to anchor my mind, will, and emotions in the safety of God. I filled my mind with His Word and kept my focus on Him. I became grateful to God for everything that was in my life. I thanked Him daily for being the God of hope and I trusted in His Word. Each day began with God, His Word, devotions and my journal. I would write my thoughts before they had a chance to be suffocated by daily activities, write prayers and most of all asking God to guide and direct my day. At the end of day I would journal all of the Blessings God had bestowed me. By doing this, when a trial would hit, I could reflect in my journal and see that God is always there.

My hope returned and I began to see Him working in my life. This gave me the ability to face the unknown of the future with positive and confident expectations of good for my life. I looked past all my circumstances and situations and was able to see the future with a confidence and hope I had never known. You can do this very same thing and your life can be totally different, and you can be a new person with a new destiny.

I remember at one point I was considering working part time for a company, which meant that I would need to place my clients on other days.

The days I would have clients, I would be slammed with absolutely no break during the day and my day began at 4:00 a.m. The more I prayed about it, I knew it would take time away from God because I would have been so exhausted that my spare time would be catching up on sleep. I had done this in the past, by placing the world before God, but not this time. His Word promises that He will provide for all of our needs. I knew financially this was going to be tough, but I believed on His promise. Reading and walking it out are two different things. Practice what you read and you will see His blessings.

Now is the time for you to bloom! Now is the time for you to rise up out of the ashes that may surround you, may have overtaken you, and may even totally consume you this very moment. Now is the time for you to break free from anything or anyone who has been holding you back, and allow your life to begin reflecting and lining up with your desires and dreams. Being isolated so that God may work in your life and you make changes, is not a bad thing. I spent many a day and night, and also holidays, alone.

This does strengthen you. You, just as I did, may have to look in the mirror and see that you yourself have been the person who has been holding you and your life back. You may have to own the fact that your mind and heart have been filled with doubts, fears, anxieties, pessimism, shame, condemnation, or hopelessness for a very long time. You may have indeed become your own worst enemy. It is time to replace the old negative voices with empowering words and thoughts in your life. This can help transform you and free you to be your true self. It is now time to allow positive thoughts to bloom which will open your mind to gratitude and blessings. The more you act upon and practice what you desire to achieve, the more you will believe that you can indeed change and reach the goals and dreams in your heart. When you catch yourself in a mental downward spiral or some form of self-condemnation, distract yourself by helping someone else. Helping others always will help to take the focus off of yourself, and you will truly feel blessed by giving to and helping others. It is also extremely important to surround yourself with friends and relationships that are very supportive, uplifting, and encouraging.

It is so important for you to know that you are valuable, blessed with dignity, full of life, and can be a shining light to this very dark world. You were born to make a positive contribution to this world, to spend your life helping and encouraging others, and to exhaust all the gifts God has bestowed upon you. You were created as one who is outstanding, an original, and one marvelous in God's eyes. You are a masterpiece created by God. As God's masterpiece, you are unique in your own way. Just like no two snowflakes are exactly alike, no other person is exactly like you. You have so much to offer others. God does not see you the way you see yourself. God does not look upon your outward appearance as the world does or even as you may have a tendency to do. He looks at your heart and soul. You have so much to give of yourself and to offer with your life. Life is one long journey similar to a road that is straight often, has many steep places, several winding turns, and even at times has what appears to be one dead-end right after another. Life can be full of heartaches, disappointments, joys, and challenging moments that all can teach you lessons which will propel you to your ultimate destination.

Pain is a great teacher yet it is often through pain that you will find your purpose in life. As you face your pain, you will later look back at those hard moments and be able to see them as blessings in disguise which gave you strength and lead you to much personal growth. You will see that God was guiding and directing your path all along. How you react to the pain in your life can either accelerate your progress or mire you down, just as if you were stuck in quicksand. Getting mired down in quicksand will usually cause people to miss out on some really amazing blessings that life has for them. Do everything you can to keep moving through your pain to avoid getting stuck in any form of emotional, relational, or circumstantial quicksand. Pain will not kill you and will actually make you a much stronger and tougher person. When encountering tough situations and painful circumstances, listen to the Holy Spirit as He guides and leads you and know that the Holy Spirit has your best interest at heart. In your moments of doubt and uncertainty have the faith to trust God. God will never let you down.

Being an outstanding person is just that, a person who stands out. God created you to stand out. God has given you many gifts with an engraved invitation to use them often. You have to choose to use them however. Even if you have not been using the gifts God has given you, it is never too late to begin using them. Your gifts still reside within you, even though they may have been dormant for a while. Using the gifts God has uniquely given you will take you into the Promised Land for your life. However, you must have the courage and boldness to abandon the old worn out paths you have been traveling, sometimes circling the same mountains and areas over and over again. It is imperative to continue following your heart and the passions inside you. Passions help develop discipline, diligence, and the perseverance to keep going forward during the tough times. Never forget that God will open the needed doors for you on your journey. He will help you fulfill the yearnings, desires, and passions that prevail in your heart.

As you tap into and utilize your strengths and gifts as you make your life's journey, it is so important to be flexible, to maintain an open mind, and to be discerning of and sensitive to your feelings and emotions. Do not allow the feelings and emotions of fear to paralyze you. When fear rears its ugly head, be intentional in creating a new cycle of thinking. These new and positive thoughts will form a new track for your mind to travel as you are realizing the amazing person God has created you to be. Never forget that God is a very skillful designer. He doesn't make junk. You are the crowning masterpiece of His work because you were created in His image. Remember that when you entered the world God looked at you and said: "You are spectacular. I am well pleased with you!"

You must begin right now to bloom out of the ashes right where you are planted. Do not wait for the perfect situation or for a safe plan to appear. If you do, you may never even try, because the fear of failure may totally consume and paralyze you. Just start. Begin with a small plan. Each day take little steps, and you will begin to see a difference as well as make progress. You are now in motion and moving forward. You will grow with each new experience. God will guide you and may even interrupt your plan at times to redirect you if you get off course or take the wrong path. Expect miracles along the way as you proceed to your desired target and goal. As you proceed on your journey, abandon any rearview mirrors you may have collected and are still using as a security blanket or to keep you focused on your past. Any gaze into the past is most always unproductive, produces unhealthy regrets, and is rarely of any benefit to you. Set your face and your entire heart and soul forward with a hope and optimism grounded in your faith. Never waver in your courage, hope, and faith. Know deep in your heart that God has provided the peace you need, and He will lead and guide you into victory and success in your life's journey.

Connected Heart

Let's begin this on another WOW, factor. Oh yeah, keep reading.

A cool Saturday morning after a Friday evening of listening and journaling notes from Dr. Jim Richards messages: Making Choices, First Impulse, Matrix of Life and What I Look Like In My Dreams.

These were on my heart so I forwarded the Impact Ministries website to a friend. Okay, keep this in mind as we move forward. We had gotten sideways with each other and had not spoken in a few weeks. Everyone has experienced those quiet times of not speaking to someone because of hurt feelings and not going to budge because the stubborn side is saying, they can apologize first. Eventually, one will take the initiative to make amends. Come on admit it. You know that this is true and happens all the time. I have to admit that I was forwarding this information, but I had not said I was sorry. Sometimes the actions speak louder than words and by taking the initiative, it was an apology. So as it goes, I attached a note which read:

> There is no hidden agenda for sending this, just information that will help propel you in life if you will truly walk this out. Believe, it comes from your heart not head and faith is just that. Your heart! Truly hopes this helps and no response is necessary because this is sent for you.

The e-mail was sent successfully. My hope was that the website would generate something in his heart to pull him out of despair.

Another prompting came shortly after the first e-mail had been sent. The second read:

> If the heart isn't different walking with worldly gains....nothing will be different. It will seem as though life is great, money in the

> bank, a relationship and life rolling along with the world by the tail. Then all of a sudden the bottom falls out because we are going through life on our own and not with the Holy Spirit guiding our decisions. Been there, done that and received the certificate. Lol.

Again, e-mail sent successfully.

I went to get coffee and sit down to finally read my daily devotion by Charles Stanley and spend time getting into the word. Comfy on the sofa, I opened it to see the title, "Developing a Tender Heart." WOW, talking about God-Incidence. Allow me to give you briefly what this said.

> The Lord wants to give each of us a "heart of flesh: so that we will be pliable and responsive to Him. When touched by the finger of God, a tender heart yields to the pressure and assumes the form He desires. To aid in this process God has sent the Holy Spirit to indwell each believer and awaken responsiveness in him or her. By yielding to the Spirit's prompting with ready obedience, the heart becomes increasingly tender and sensitive to His leading. Any resistance to God will result in hardening. People with tender hearts stay closely connected to the body of Christ seeking to build up and encourage others in their walk of faith.
>
> As He pokes His finger into each hard area, listen to His instructions, and rely on the Spirit's power to help you yield and obey. Let Him shape you into a beautiful and useful vessel.

Talking about timing. I had just taken the first step to communicate and hoping that he would be receptive to the information and then read this.

So again, with amazement, I sent a third e-mail.

I know you may be thinking, poor soul that is on the receiving end. So this one read:

> WOW, I just sent other e-mails offering encouragement and writing in my journal as an attempt to be a blessing to you versus holding bitterness in my heart. Then I open the devotion to read the message which seemed directed to our situation and find all the goodness in this. Can we say Holy Spirit's direction? He is our guide.

I attached the devotion with this note and pressed send.

"For everything there is a season; and a time for every matter under heaven." Ecclesiastes 3:1 (ESV)

"And let us not grow weary of doing good, for in due season we will reap, if we do not give up." Galatians 6:9 (ESV)

Had I known his heart was hardened and he would have deleted the information, I would not have sent it. His heart, being the soil, would have received absolutely nothing from this, but I did know that he was studying the word of God and his heart was prepared. Not only that, I had to humble myself by sending this. Yes, he could have rejected me and the information, but I knew I needed to take that step of faith and allow God to work in his heart. Being vulnerable is a scary feeling and not knowing if you will be reprimanded, but that is the enemy toying with your thoughts. God is one of peace, not confusion and piece by piece this puzzle came together.

Awake the Heart!

A God Sized Dream

A God size dream is one that you know, you cannot accomplish on your own. They seem so far out of reach, that you may want to dismiss them before you ever begin.

On January 1, 2015 God placed a dream in my heart of writing a devotional. He gave me the title and the contents that would reach the hurting. I was thinking, He must have the wrong person because I am not an "eloquent writer." What a sense of humor. But, I knew He had something big in mind and He would receive the glory.

"All Scripture is given by inspiration of God…" 2 Timothy 3:16

Another name for scripture is our Bible that we read today and many men were the writers inspired by the Holy Spirit.

After the dream was placed on my heart, I shared this with a few friends. We prayed about it and they not only confirmed that this was a great idea, but said that God would lead me to write again after the completion of the devotional. I was thinking, yeah right, I have not even given this a lot of thought and you are thinking that far in advance. A friend offered to edit this when completed and I felt the energy from our conversation to move forward.

We all have dreams for our life and for some, these are different than others. God will open the door, but sometime we just do not see it and miss a great opportunity.

I was determined to work on this devotional and use this as a tool to touch a life, give hope and inspire others to continue moving forward. My writing was daily, and some days the words would flow with ease then I would encounter the writer's block when I could barely write a sentence.

I would get discouraged at times and want to stop. At least I was moving forward and God was providing the thoughts and words to transcribe into the book.

There would be times at 3:00 or 4:00 a.m., the Holy Spirit would place thoughts in my mind, but when you are sleeping you try to assess real or a dream. Trying to open my eyes, pull myself out of a fog and sit up was effort. After waking, I immediately knew the words I was hearing were intended for a particular devotion I had been working on. Sometimes I would get out of bed and begin to write and other times I would just jot this down in a notebook and back to sleep again. When the Holy Spirit moves, you need to listen. Driving and there would be thoughts, so I would pull off the road and text myself what He had placed on my heart, as a reminder.

It seemed my spare time was spent writing, but that was fine because it was winter months and cold. The writing seemed slow because it took me longer to think through what would reach and inspire the readers. Writing a paragraph then go back and review to find I was not pleased with it and scratch that for a rewrite. That happened quite often, but God was giving me the words and what He wanted placed that touched a life.

After two months of writing consistently, the devotional was complete. I contacted my friend that graciously offered to edit this for me. This took a few days to get it in his hands, and after he had it an uneasy feeling was placed on my heart. At first I dismissed it, until the feeling became stronger that I needed to get this back. I did and shortly after knew that this was in the wrong hands. Not having anything to do with my friend that was editing, but due to outside forces that would have sabotaged the work.

Now what? I was not sure what to do at this point and was disappointed that it was not going to work out. After praying about it, the Holy Spirit placed on my heart to have friends that I had not thought about to edit it. One was a retired teacher and the other had been in ministry for years. This was ideal and a blessing from God. He was indeed directing my path.

Now it was in their hands and there was not a rush for completion. After they began to read, they asked me if I was sure about releasing it. Why would I not want to, after spending two months and all of my spare time writing, sure I did. The editing began and several of the daily devotions complete. Then it was almost as though I had forgotten about it or it was no longer a priority as originally thought. Looking at the pages that were edited, I began to pray about this and search for answers. What was I to gain from this dream? Why would God place this on my heart so clear and then put a halt to it?

God was walking me through times in my life of painful affliction and tough trials, strengthening and healing me. He had opened the door for me to write and given me the words, but the words were for me changing me in so many ways and to become more dependent upon Him.

He was preparing me with courage and victory to serve Him in 2016. I would not forget what He had done with my writings and He was showing me that I could do anything I set my mind to. Being obedient, I see more and more doors opening. Remember at the beginning of this, I shared how meeting with a friend he said I would not only write the devotional, but God would lead me to write again.

March 2016, God did open a door for me to write again. I was invited to submit a chapter for the book *Beyond the Woman*, but I was not confident in writing, so I declined. Marilyn Rodriguez asked me again to reconsider writing the chapter. She had complete confidence in me and knew that I could do this. I accepted, submitted my chapter and I was elated to announce that on March 15, 2016 *Beyond the Woman* became a #1 Bestseller Internationally and USA.

God was preparing me in 2015 for the calling to Co-author this book. He had provided me with the abilities to write and I was not going to allow the enemy to steal the plans God has for my life to reach others. The enemy had won so many times before with thoughts of fear and doubt, but not this time. I was taking that step of faith and knew that God would carry me the rest of the way with His resources, not of my own.

To my amazement, people will be happy to strap into a zip line, parasail or bungee jump without knowing any real safety precautions/dangers and at the hands of total strangers, but they will not trust the one that created you, God. God has your best interest at heart, you belong to Him. A stranger does not care about your well being.

"I know your deeds. See, I have placed before you an open door that no one can shut. I know that you have little strength, yet you have kept my word and have not denied my name." Revelation 3:8 (NIV)

The open door is so that we may share Jesus Christ with others. "Those who try to hang on when God is trying to move on will always be miserable." Joyce Meyer

You may be missing out on great opportunities if you are not listening for God's voice in every aspect of your life. Be willing to leave your plans behind when He invites you to join Him in a wondrous journey.

"In their hearts humans plan their course, but the Lord establishes their steps." Proverbs 16:9 (NIV)

Nothing is Accidental

Always God's Timing

A cold morning, temperature 21 degrees and the bed is so warm and comfortable. Nice that this is a morning I do not have to get up at 4:00 a.m. and get to sleep in. Well, I guess not. The Holy Spirit was prompting me to get up. He always seems to work with me in times when I really would like to sleep. I guess that is the best time because it is quiet and I don't have the noise of the day occupying my thoughts.

Against my will, I get out of the bed, dress in something comfortable and warm, then on to the kitchen for coffee. Half asleep and waiting for the coffee to brew, it is all I can do to stay awake. Coffee is ready, Jesus and I enjoy creamer in ours, now to the sofa turning on TBN (Trinity Broadcasting Network) to find Joel Osteen's message.

Hang tight here comes the confirmation.

Years ago it was on my heart to begin a Women's Ministry to teach ladies how to live life as a sermon and one for the broken hearted. Then was not the right time, but in February of 2016 this seemed to be the time and I began writing each weekly message or at least how I thought it would go. God can change that order, this is just a draft.

Even though I had this in my heart, I truly did not have the resources to begin because it meant giving up needed income. Well, the Holy Spirit was pulling me out of my comfort zone with another direction, and this was this book. I had already been writing for the ministry, but along with that came messages that were dear to me that life is not a coincidence. I would begin to write briefly, more like notes and blessings of situations where it was so obvious that it was truly God. My eyes were opened to situations around me that were positively God at work. I wanted to share those with others, but not thinking it would evolve into a book. God chose otherwise to move me with this.

Stepping out of the comfort zone does place you into uncharted territory and the enemy loves to remind you of how unqualified you are to carry this through. Bringing powerful thoughts of past mistakes and even mistakes made after becoming saved. To the point you are ready to throw in the towel before you begin.

I admit, I do consider myself unqualified when it comes to writing because that is not something I consider to be gifted with. It is very much a challenge to sit down and have my writing flow and have the tendency to watch others as they write so eloquently and with ease. But God knew there was something to share and reach others that may be going through similar situations, circumstances of life, God-Incidences when they thought were coincidences etc.

Here is the gut of the message:

When something is small in our heart, it is huge to God. We may not have resources or seem to have enough talent, but God is bigger. God will give you everything. Never look at the "Not Enough" attitude, that will stop the process that God has for you. In the flesh, we wait for everything to be in alignment before we take the first step.

Look at the disciples feeding 5,000. They were in a remote area and it was late. The disciples were dismissing the crowd to find something to eat. Jesus told them, "You give them something to eat."

The disciples had five loaves and two fish. Jesus directed them to have all the people sit down in groups of hundreds and fifties. They took the bread and fish, looking to heaven and giving thanks, broke the loaves. They all ate and were satisfied.

If you will give Him your ordinary, He will make it extraordinary. Don't focus on the problem or something negative, it will only magnify.

Talking about a confirmation! If I had not gotten up and turned this on, I probably would have missed this message that gives hope to move forward.

"When you step out of your comfort zone you will learn how to navigate in your new season." T. D. Jakes

God stirs hearts of many today, but are we willing to step out of our comfort zone to make a difference and reach others for His kingdom? It may be taking someone to lunch, sending a special note, helping a neighbor or being involved in ministry, but God wants us to have a heart to serve Him. A lot of the time we will not make that step for fear of the unknown and then we allow excuses to creep in. By not facing your fears, you remain in bondage and that is exactly where the enemy has you. Holding you back and shrinking into a daily routine of comfort.

The Holy Spirit is our comforter and has us when we step out in faith.

God uses the broken and unqualified, and equips them…

> My grace is sufficient for you, for my power is made perfect in weakness." Therefore I will boast all the more gladly about my weaknesses, so that Christ's power may rest on me. That is why, for Christ's sake, I delight in weaknesses, in insults, in hardships, in persecutions, in difficulties . For when I am weak, then I am strong.

2 Corinthians 12:9-11 (NIV)

Time Sensitive

Have you ever received mail stamped "time sensitive"? Sometimes that is how we see prayers, and they are answered in a timely manner.

God's timing is not our timing. We want to blame God for not answering quickly, but we also need to take a look at what we are praying for.

Are we asking randomly and selfishly? Is this to get us out of a bind so that we may return to selfish behavior? Search scripture that applies to your prayer requests, does this align?

We think we know what is best for our lives, but God knows differently. I remember praying that God would bring a wonderful man into my life. I even had close friends praying and I remember a dear friend telling me one day, as I was frustrated, "It isn't time, you aren't ready and God knows you aren't healed." She was right. Had there been someone in my life during the two years I was praying, I would not have grown closer to God. The relationship would have been a distraction during this time. God had a work to do in my life and to grow me, but I was so exhausted with feeling lonely. I had allowed those thoughts to consume me.

What God was doing during those two years was to open my eyes to what "I didn't want" in my life and not to settle for someone that did not share the same path. That person of course was not going to be an exact match, but I was taking a closer look as to what God wanted for my life. In other words, my "picker" was broken when selecting someone with the qualities that were encouraging, uplifting, would be respectful and leading me with a greater walk in God. Hard to swallow those words, that I needed a work in me. Were there times I was ready to give up? Yes, but it was giving up my own search and allowing God to bring him into my life. I was standing in my own way and God was not going to intervene until I relinquished control.

God was not going to answer a prayer if it brought temptation into my life. My heart was changing and He knew that. The one to answer my prayer was God and Him alone. Not everyone I was running to asking for advice and counsel on what to do.

He may be delaying an answer because it seems like a hand out and not genuine. It is all for self when we cannot even offer help to others.

He may have us in a "holding pattern" until we learn to listen and His call to be obedient. There was one night during the Christmas holidays I was going to meet friends for dinner and to celebrate together. I had taken time to select the perfect outfit, matching jewelry, shoes and handbag for the occasion. I arrived at the time everyone agreed upon, but I waited in my car for the others to arrive before going in. I had waited 15 minutes and they still had not arrived. The longer I waited the more I thought, I did not want to do this. The Holy Spirit was nudging me to leave. I had a sense this was not a fit for me, at least this particular evening. As it turned out, it would not have been. I was so glad that night, that I followed my heart. I love my friends, but making the decision to follow the Holy Spirit was wise. So what I am telling you is that you are always faced with choices.

Recently during the process of writing this book, I was faced with a difficult choice. I had already made plans, with a friend, for a brief mini-vacation to the beach. It was either stay home and work on the book, placing God first or enjoying the sun and sand of the beach. So tempting to go on and relax, but God came first. The beach would be there later. My friend was very upset with my decision and did not speak to me afterward. Yes, my feelings were very hurt. Placing God first may not be the most popular choice among your friends, but will be rewarding.

I received this from a dear friend after sharing what happened and it read:

> Tina, holding onto one thing always requires letting go of another. I'm sorry you missed the beach, but not sorry you chose a higher purpose. Congrats! The beach will be waiting for you when you're ready.

That could not have come at a better time. God knew I needed comforting words. Profound!

God also enjoys hearing prayers that we may think are trivial, such as a lawn mower cranking. Yes, I have been outside pulling the cord several times trying to get it to crank and nothing. I shared with God that if He wanted me to cut the grass, then I needed the mower to start. Next pull, started up.

The enemy will make prayer seem meaningless, especially when delayed. He will have you thinking it is a waste of time and not effective or that only good things happen to good people. What we have from God is by grace and He gives gifts to all, but the enemy wants us frustrated and confused. God loves us and wants the best for us, so when He answers He knows exactly what we need. Being obedient, does draw us closer to God but not by fear. We do this because we love Him and want a relationship with Him.

Have confidence and patience when waiting on answers. God loves to surprise us!

Living Life Motivational Videos

The idea to touch lives and make a difference through videos, began in June 2016. Again, not a coincidence, but one of God. I had just completed writing the manuscript of *It's Not Odd It Is God*, in May, when the nudging to begin the video series was on my heart. Speaking to an audience whether live or by camera, has never been easy for me. This is outside of my comfort zone and God would truly need to lead me with this. He had already done a work in me by writing the manuscript because I certainly didn't feel qualified. So, I trusted He would carry me through with each video message and calm the jitters when speaking.

"For my thoughts are not your thoughts, neither are your ways my ways" declares the Lord." Isaiah 55:8

"I pray that out of his glorious riches he may strengthen you with power through his spirit in your inner being." Ephesians 3:16 NIV

How was I going to accomplish what God had asked me to do? I had never filmed a video before and knew nothing of the makings. Truly 'green' at this. But when God places an idea in your heart, he will pave the way. Opening doors with right people and providing guidance. A teacher. He is fully aware of your needs.

"Consider the ravens: they neither sow nor reap they have neither storehouse nor barn and yet God feeds them. Of how much more value are you than the birds!" Luke 12:24 ESV

This must have been His plan because, through mutual friends, I was connected to Sonia Lamique from Uruguay.. Sonia's talents range from journalism to radio broadcasting and film editing. God had been working behind the scenes, connecting the dots meeting the right people and preparing my heart, for many months before I met Sonia. There is a purpose when God brings a person in your life. This is to fulfill His plan.

After many conversations about this project, together we had a plan to begin. Sonia would be traveling to the United States in August 2016, meeting with other businesses and worked her schedule to visit Alabama. We would only have a few weeks to film before her returning to Uruguay. My part was to have the topics and the 'meat' of these videos prepared so that we could film several messages per day. The goal was to record 2-3 per day and build our library so that when she returned to Uruguay, we could pull from the storage.

Sonia arrived in August as planned and, due to preparation on both parts, filming was smooth and successful. This went off without a hitch, and at least ten topics were recorded. Because we had these stored, when Sonia returned home it was easy for the two of us to collaborate on design ideas for each message and timing for uploading to YouTube. Even though the recordings were successful and the messages clear, I just felt that they were so rehearsed and stiff. My gut feeling, was that something was missing.

After giving much thought to this project, I decided to take a break from recording for a few months and just be still and wait for God's guidance. What He showed me during this time, was to be 'real' and speak from my heart. Let others see me relaxed in front of the camera and sometimes that meant fumbling my words and losing my train of thought. But, that was okay because I was speaking with emotion and feelings. No longer constrained by a straight jacket of perfectionism. When I let go and let God have this, I began to feel more comfortable in front of the camera and the words began to flow more naturally and with ease. So what would that mean for the original videos and how would I record the new ones. God led me to Amy Cotten, who is a close friend. So I contacted Sonia and shared my new vision for this project and she agreed that Amy would be perfect to record. Sonia then sent specific instructions on how to record a successful video. In the beginning, Amy and I would have a few takes before the final one was acceptable for the public. We worked so well together and our time seemed effortless, yet powerful with the presence of God. I no longer felt like I was settling for a partial fulfillment. God was there. Allow me to share.

There was a video I felt strongly about and this was speaking on 'words of life and death.' Words can encourage or discourage. The tongue is very powerful and can destroy, if not bridled. I just could not get this off my mind and the words continued to play over and over in my head.

On a Friday afternoon, very cloudy and rain all around, Amy and I set out to record. The recording went without a hitch, and we were finished. Sonia received the video the same evening and began editing. This is what Sonia noticed:

> Tina, 1 minute, 7 seconds into the video, a light descends to the right side of you. This is not an effect of the camera because it is outside and without artificial light. This is something incredible. The light has the power of divinity. God and the angels are compared with light. You used the power of words and the light appeared. Friday, April 21, 2017.

Reference to Angels: Acts 1:11, Acts 12:7-11, Acts 8:26, Acts 10:3, 7, 22, Acts 27:23-24

Again, allowing God to take over and releasing my grip to control, He was able to steer the course of each message. Amy and I were preparing to record the Current of Life video one Summer morning and because I had released control, God was showing me His awesomeness through creativity. God not only provided the title and message weeks prior to shooting, but opened my eyes to the location and how others would view this. Not only would the audience hear the message, but they would experience this as well. The location was a large creek area located near a greenway. Because it is a greenway, there is a lot of activity, which means background noise, and we couldn't have that in the video. This is a distraction when trying to hear the message. Amy and I both decided it would be best to record early on a Saturday morning, which worked for our schedules and before the walkers hit the trail. So that is what we did. We met about 7:30 a.m. on a Saturday and, walked along the creek until we could find the perfect place where the water was flowing across the rocks, a good current, and also easy access from the trail. We made our way to the water and across we went. Amy was a little more to the bank side and I actually walked across finding where the water would flow downstream demonstrating the current. We both were now sitting in the water and ready to record. Yes, we are in the water. Amy, when preparing to record, will count to three and that is my cue to begin. She does her usual count and I freeze. Not because I wasn't prepared, but I felt in my heart the Holy Spirit was redirecting the words for this message. I asked Amy if it would be okay to pause for prayer and then just wait. That is exactly what we did. Both sitting in this creek, quietly and waiting. I am sure if there had been someone to pass they would have thought we were two crazy women. After a few minutes, I felt that peace and was ready. When I began to speak, the words truly flowed and the message took a different turn than what I had prepared for. Amy and I both could feel His presence guiding us through this message.

After the video was released, a friend began asking questions about the location and if we had actually waded across the creek. I shared that we had found the opening off of the trail and we did have to walk through trees and down rocks to the water. This is what she said, "You do know that creek is full of water moccasins?" I didn't, but I sure did at that moment. I am terrified of snakes. A hedge of protection was around us that day. God had something to say!

When you have a dream, don't settle for second best. Keep your eyes on the big picture and continue to guard this. God wants to fulfill your dreams!

A Dream Became Reality

Dreams are a part of our life and some of these we remember from our sleep. Dreaming is a natural part of life with both believers and non-believers; therefore we need to understand if they are of God or a dream that was on our mind.

One thing to ask yourself, 'does it match God's character?'. If the dream is telling you to commit a sin, it clearly is not God. The Bible repeatedly mentions visions, which were in a dream like state.

"Hear my words: If there is a prophet among you, I the Lord make myself known to him in a vision; I speak with him in a dream." Numbers 12:6. (ESV)

Also, go to God in prayer and ask him to reveal the nature of the dream. Just as Daniel was shown, what is He trying to show you?

"Then the mystery was revealed to Daniel in a vision of the night. Then Daniel blessed the God in heaven." Daniel 2:19 (ESV)

My dream began in a deep sleep, July 21,2016. Rarely did I remember details of a dream, but on this particular morning, as I awoke, I remembered everything. So excited about all the details, I got out of bed, made my way to the sofa, this is where my daily journal was placed and began writing. It was 4:00 a.m. and I knew I needed to write quickly so that I could get ready for the gym, but all the details of the dream were flooding my mind. As I would write, more and more became clear.

Follow me through the dream.

I met a tall handsome gentleman with brown hair, wearing a white button down shirt, jeans and western style boots. I was speaking to a friend when I noticed him. He did not seem that interested in speaking with me, or so I thought, but it turned out that he was just shy. As I began talking with him, he said "I can see into your heart through your eyes."

Time seemed like it stood still until our conversation picked up about a building. I noticed a building with a western type star hanging on the door. I asked him, "Do you live here?" He replied, "I built this, it has two rooms, but I do not live here."

I awoke to the sound of my alarm and wondering what the dream was all about.

As I mentioned previously, I journaled the dream then off to the gym. When I arrived at the gym, I shared this dream with a few very close friends of which I knew would understand and they are believers as well. Together we talked about it, but really did not have a clue what God was trying to reveal. That evening I was praying, and this was my prayer "Lord I have all the details of this dream. I do not know what this means and how will I know him. Please guide me Lord."

The Holy Spirit said this; "You will know him when you see him."

I was anxiously waiting for days following the dream, to meet this man, but nothing happened. Then I forgot about it.

A dear friend wanted me to meet a man that she knew and thought we had common interests. I agreed, so she forwarded my number to him and we began talking. After several conversations, we both decided it was time to meet in person. He invited me to church, which was great. But, I was apprehensive about trying to find him at the church so I would meet him at his house and we would ride together.

It was August 21, 2016. One month to the date of my dream. I was so nervous while driving to actually see him. I had only seen pictures and we know pictures do not always tell the whole story. I pull into the driveway, park the car and try to calm my nerves as I get out and make my way to the door.

The front door was open with only the glass storm door between us. A little knock and I see him approaching the door. A tall handsome man with brown hair, white button down shirt, jeans and western style boots. Could this be the man from the dream, I asked myself? He opened the door and I was shocked. I asked him, "Do you normally wear this to church?" His reply, "I do wear jeans often but I do not know why today I decided to wear the white button down with the jeans and boots."

My eyes were huge.

We got in the car leave for the church service and I was thinking about the dream. When service let out, as we were exiting the row and waiting for the crowd to clear, he turned and said "I can see your heart through your eyes."

You could have knocked me over with a feather. Just like the dream. We went to eat lunch and then back to his house, so that I could get my car and head home.

When we arrived back, he said, "Before you leave I would like you to see the landscaping around the backyard." We went out back and there was a building with the western style star hanging on the door. I asked him, "How long has this building been here?" Reply, "I just finished it. It has two rooms, but I do not live here."

The dream that began July 21, 2016 became reality August 21, 2016. God places people in your life for a reason. God had a plan for us meeting, even though it was brief. You see, he was struggling to walk a new path of life. Our meeting gave him hope and strength.

God always has a plan!

"And it shall come to pass afterward that I will pour out my Spirit on all flesh; your sons and daughters shall prophesy, your old men shall dream dreams and your young men shall see visions." Joel 2:27 (ESV)

The Comfort of Angels

Angel means messenger of God.

The two stories you are about to read are amazing and very similar, as God sent His messenger to comfort. My prayer is that this gives you peace and hope.

My brother was married with two children, but had struggled with life in general, for years. It seemed like a roller coaster. Everything would click along smoothly for months, before the bottom would fall out. During the times he would be in a pit, he would go into isolation from friends and family in order to protect himself from questions. Each time he hit a low, he seemed to be able to work it out. The process was slow, but every day there was progress until he leveled out. The confidence would build, like he could conquer the world. I remember one time, he slipped to the point of almost losing his job when God sent an angel to protect him, walk with him and get him back on his feet. That lasted about a year before he relapsed and did lose his job. This took a toll on him as well as the family. I watched the feelings of hopelessness, persistent sadness and emptiness take over his life.

When you have a loved one going through something like this and they cannot see the light at the end of the tunnel, you honestly do not know what to do except offer support of being there and listening. I would listen and think there was a glimmer of hope, but the negative emotions would occupy his mind.

I received a call on a Friday morning while I was at the gym. He asked me to come and talk with him. Knowing he was depressed, I asked him to please not do anything and give me time to get there. I remember praying as I was driving to see him, that he would not do anything.

As I approached his driveway, I could see the back door was open and thinking to myself, "God please let him be okay because I cannot handle something happening to him." He was sitting in the kitchen and there was a loaded gun on the table. We talked for about 30 minutes and then I asked him to please unload the gun, it made me nervous and I was very uncomfortable around guns. He did and placed it back on the table.

He then began pouring his heart out to me about what a failure he was to himself and those he loved. He could not see a light at the end of the tunnel only more trains barreling down the track. The depression had turned to thoughts of suicide. We talked longer and I had told him that I could not sit with him 24/7 to guard and protect him, but to please talk with God and get his life straight. God would help him. When I left, he said, "I love you and you have always listened to me, but this will probably be the last time you see me." I told him I loved him and did not want to acknowledge what he had just said.

When I left, I was praying he would not follow through with his thoughts, but I had a sense that he would. I did not speak with him again after that, but my parents had and they said he was back to his normal happy self. I should have known with that sudden switch, from being very sad to calm, that he would take his life.

The Wednesday morning following our talk, at 3:00 a.m. he took his life. I did not receive the call until 6:00 a.m. Then I went straight to his home. Our family pastor arrived shortly after, and I remember saying that I just wanted to know if he was in heaven or hell because he had suffered so much off and on for years. It was not so much the grieving for his loss because I knew he was no longer in misery, but I wanted the confirmation he was at home with the Lord.

The pastor said that I would not know that. When he told me that I could feel the hair stand on my neck. I was so upset because I wanted to have peace in my heart for him. I was not angry at the response; my comfort would be to know that he was no longer suffering and resting in heaven.

Recalling his death was on a Wednesday at 3:00 a.m. Thursday morning at 3:00 a.m. I awoke from a dead sleep, to see him standing by my bed. As I sat up, he held his hand out and said, "I am okay."

I never shared this with anyone because they would have thought I was crazy, or my vision was satanic.

The memorial service was Friday and after the service, his daughter (which was 12 at the time) told me that she had a dream on Thursday at the exact same time her father had passed away. I asked her to share the vision. She described exactly what I had seen and I had not shared this with anyone. This was all God and not a coincidence. He was comforting both of us in different ways

Years had passed after losing my brother and I was going through a difficult time, wishing he was with me. It was during the hot summer months, when temperatures were high and humidity even higher. I went to sit on the front porch at about 10:00 p.m. It was very quiet and peaceful out, but uncomfortable with the warm weather. As I sat in a rocking chair, I looked up and saw one star that lit up the sky. The star was shining so brightly.

I began talking to my brother, saying how much I wish he were here and could be with me. No sooner than the words came out of my mouth, a very cool breeze (like a fan blowing) came across me and my chair began to rock. I knew he was with me, an angel comforting me. I went to visit my parents the next morning and the first thing my father said, "Did you see the sky last night? There was only one star and it was shining so brightly, like a night light."

Only God!

Losing Laura

My precious friend lost her beautiful daughter Laura in a car accident on December 19, 2001. This day will always be engraved in her heart.

When Laura married she said, "I do" to her husband and gained a stepson. Her stepson was a "bonus" son. This story takes place during the Christmas season and Laura loved this time of year. As my friend shares, it was a typical Monday at work and she was exhausted, but there was a nudge for her to stop by and visit Laura before going home. So she decided to stop by and visit. Laura with her "bonus" son, were sitting in the floor wrapping gifts for Christmas. "I will never forget that beautiful smile as she was so excited about the holidays. This smile will be forever etched in my mind. Little did I know this would be the last time I would see her."

On Wednesday morning Laura dropped her "bonus" son off at school. As she approached a stop sign the sun was blinding and she thought it was clear to cross, but when she did an oncoming truck hit her in the driver's door and she was killed instantly. Angels were all around. The officer that was called to the scene was a close friend of the family. When she was contacted about losing Laura it was her very best friend who went to tell her. As her friend arrived to give her the sad news, she had also asked God to allow her to share this burden as well. Be careful what you ask for because her friend walked this out with her for almost a year.

The usual stages of grief had begun, the first being shock. "I felt like being in a movie only I was on the outside looking in." I felt like I was alone, but I was not because I was surrounded by close friends. Close friends are wonderful, but if you have never experienced a loss like this you know that they cannot begin to understand what you are dealing with and how deeply your heart is broken. Not just broken, but torn in a million pieces and trying to understand why God would allow this to happen and take her.

Several months had gone by and she was taking one day at a time. She recalls a vision she had at this time:

> Being in a dead sleep I awoke to see Laura and this is what she said "I am okay. I want my husband to be happy and find someone to share his life." What an amazing peace and relief that I received from this. I did not share this with many because I knew they would think I was crazy.
>
> Although I felt peace in my heart, I still could not understand why she was taken at an early age.

So she began attending grief classes and through these classes found that there would be a large conference held in Atlanta on grief and how to cope. With encouragement from friends, she decided to attend. While attending sessions, she found that many experience the same type of visions and this is not uncommon, a gift from God.

As she said:

> Being a Christian helps you when you are struggling to find strength and comfort, but it does not take away the pain of losing

a loved one. The grieving process takes time and you repeat the steps of this over and over. Eventually, by the grace of God you find a new and normal happy life.

As the song "The Dance" goes, "it was worth the pain."

Because she had twent-three wonderful years with her precious daughter. As she shared Laura's story she also said that looking back she could see the presence of God before, during and after the loss.

"But Jesus called the children to him and said, 'Let the little children come to me, and do not hinder them, for the kingdom of God belongs to such as these.'" Luke 18:16 (NIV)

These are not coincidences, only God. Angels are messengers of God's presence that portray love, protection and justice. Angels are never intended as a fascination, but to know that God is with us and the one who sends them.

"Are not all angels ministering spirits sent to save those who will inherit salvation?" Hebrews 1:14 (NIV)

Angels visit us and we may not even realize it. This may be a stranger, a ministering spirit for believers, when we are in desperate times and facing obstacles.

"For he shall give his angels charge over thee, to keep thee in all my ways." Psalm 91:11 (NIV)

Hope in our Valleys

> A Psalm of David. The Lord is my shepherd, I shall not want. He makes me lie down in green pastures. He leads me beside the still water. He restores my soul. He leads me in paths of righteousness for his name's sake. Even though I walk through the valley of the shadow of death, I will fear no evil, for you are with me, your rod and your staff, they comfort me. You prepare a table before me in the presence of my enemies, you anoint my head with oil, my cup overflow…
>
> Psalm 23: 1-6 (NIV)

God brings people into our lives, whether it is for a long or short period of time, a season to help and learn from each other. There was no coincidence in the timing of meeting my new friend, but it seemed as quickly as he entered, he also walked away. We both had walked through valleys, although in different ways, we both had stories to share and the work that God had done in our lives.

Allow me to share his story of hope during difficult times.

> *Life was great. Not that there weren't the everyday problems of life, but my wife and I had five kids and we were all very involved in our church and had been on several mission trips together as a family. We were very close and enjoyed doing things together. That was the one comment we heard from other people, was how close we all were.*
>
> *In January 2011, that began to change. My wife had caught a bad cold or perhaps even the flu, so we thought. We went to the doctor a couple of times and received some medicine to try to help her with the*

flu. One night as she was coming to bed she fell to her knees and so I rushed her to the Emergency Room. In my mind was thinking, "they'll just give her an IV and release her this afternoon or tomorrow." I was somewhat surprised when the doctor told me that he was going to keep her overnight and run some tests on her.

This did not alarm me too much as I was thinking that this is probably standard procedure. I was still thinking my wife just had a bad flu until the nurse came to me and told me that if I had waited another day to bring her in she would have been in a coma. The tests revealed that my wife had a staph infection that had eaten her up on the inside.

She stayed in the hospital a month having tests run on her consistently. There was never any good news. I compare it to a 15 round boxing match and we lost every round. Having been involved in church all my life I had heard of so many miracles of God's healing people as Christians joined in prayer. That didn't happen for us. Having been in Birmingham, AL most of our lives and having been involved in a couple of churches, we had thousands of people praying for us. But we didn't get that miracle healing. My wife died in February, one month after I took her to the ER.

One of the things I learned is that the more people you have praying for you doesn't always mean your prayer will be answered. There is not always correlation between more people praying and answered prayers. I don't have God figured out.

So now what? I am without a wife and I have five teenagers who are 13-19 years old who are without their mom. One of the hardest things for a parent to go through is to see their kids hurt and there is nothing you can do for them. This is where I was. My kids were hurting and crying over the loss of their mom and I couldn't fix it for them. Besides prayer and being there with them, I was helpless.

For seven weeks, I felt like Job from the Bible. He and I became good friends. "For what I fear comes upon me, and what I dread befalls me." Job 3:25

Our worst fear had come upon us. God was silent, and I, like Job wondered why.

God began to work in my heart and remind me how He would always bring the Israelites to remember all that He had done for them when they got discouraged or would question His dealings. God would ask them, "Do you not remember how I delivered you from slavery in Egypt? Do you not remember when I parted the Red Sea for you? Do you not remember that I fed you with manna from heaven? Do you not remember how I brought you into the promised land ... a land flowing with milk and honey?"

I began to think of how God had blessed me with a good house, five healthy kids, a good job and food to eat. Even though I did not understand why God took my kids' mother, I couldn't argue that He had blessed and He did love me even though I was hurting, mad at Him and I didn't understand why my kids had to go through this pain and loss of their mom.

I began to think of all the scriptures showing me that He did love me and I had to choose whether I believed them or not even when I was hurting. I chose to believe His word even though my emotions were running contrary.

Regarding being mad at God, for some reason Christians think that it's not spiritual to be mad at God. Yet, I think scriptures show us the opposite. Job, David and Jeremiah were all godly men, but they did get angry with God when they went through hard times in their lives. They did question God. God was not shocked by their anger towards Him.

Another thing that helped me is when I went to my pastor and talked about the thousands of unanswered prayers for my wife, He told me. "God did answer your prayers. He gave your wife what was best for her." I couldn't argue with that. She had suffered and her body was badly infected and eaten up with the staph infection. Because she loved the Lord and had given her life to Him, I knew she was in heaven with Jesus and had received a new body that was whole and not sick anymore. She was much better off.

Then the pastor said something that shocked me but changed my perspective and my life. He told me, "God also gave you what was best for you." The light bulb came on I began to think, "God you could have saved my wife, but You chose not to. Therefore, Your plan for me is to raise my five kids by myself." So I told Him, "OK God, let's do it."

This changed my whole approach to what lay before me. I knew I couldn't do it by myself and He would have to help me, but I knew He would be with me because this was His plan for me.

One of the verses I went to constantly through the pain was Jeremiah 17:14 "Heal me, O Lord and I will be healed; Save me and I will be saved, for You are my praise." I cried out to Him to heal me. I knew only He could.

Once I accepted that this was God's plan for me some incredible things began to happen. I now began to have peace through the pain. And my quiet times with the Lord in the mornings were something that is hard to describe. I felt a closeness with Him like I had never felt before. I spent time reading His word and praying to Him, it felt like I was in His present. As I sat in my recliner with His word in one hand and a cup of coffee in the other, I pictured myself just sitting at His feet. I would just say to Him, "OK God, what do You want to teach me this morning?" This closeness went on for about a year.

I think He gave me this closeness with Him for strength to raise my five kids as they were dealing with the loss of their mom. Can you imagine raising five teenagers who just lost their mother? Every morning I was on my knees praying, "God I am overwhelmed. I can't do this. You have to help me." Not only were there the normal issues teens have to face, but throw in having to change schools, and coping with the death.

What was once in many ways, the All American Family, now we were faced with issues we had never dealt with before or had imagined. My kids dealt with the grief in many ways. My oldest two turned to things that this society offers them for temporary comfort. There were many other issues I had to deal with my teenage kids trying to handle the death of their mom.

For those who are single again, I offer this as a widower, who like you, went through that terrible time of loss.

These are some things that you may experience.

- *You may feel like your world had been turned upside down and you have lost all your security.*
- *Your thoughts may be confused for a period of time.*
- *You may find it hard to do even the simplest things, like paying bills. I hated the thought of having to do that.*
- *You will experience emotional swings. One minute you say you will never marry again and the next minute you want to get married tomorrow. You may want to sell your house, quit your job or take a trip away.*
- *Many more. If you have experienced these things, welcome to the club. I just wanted to tell you they are normal.*

Before all these trials started, I thought I knew what faith was. I thought I would make an A on a Faith test. I was wrong. I realized I had been in the minor leagues and now I was in the major leagues. It was time to fall at God's feet and cry for His grace. Another personal trial I experienced in addition to being a mom and dad to my kids, was that I lost my job during this time and I went 8 months looking diligently trying to find one. Another incident when I had to cry out to the Lord.

As far as my walk and my dealing with all this, first I had to choose if I believed the scriptures even though I didn't feel it or like where I was. I remember talking to God and I told Him, "God either Your word is true or it's not. Even though I don't feel it, I choose to believe You." It was a choice.

Secondly, the old saying, "it just takes time to heal" is very true. It does take time. I remember months later walking down the halls of my workplace and I caught myself whistling a song and smiling and I said, "What is this? Is this happiness that has returned?"

I began to see these verses becoming real to me, Psalm 40:1-3

1-"I waited patiently for the Lord, and He inclined to me and heard my cry."

2-"He brought me up out of the pit of destruction, out of the miry clay, and He set my feet upon a rock making my footsteps."

3-"He put a new song in my mouth, a song of praise to our God; Many will see and fear and will trust in the Lord."

I was in the pit of destruction, but God did set me upon a rock. He put a new song in my mouth. I could once again have joy, He had given my hope.

The reason I write this to you is to let you know, no matter how bad the trial is, there is hope because of who God is. He will put a new song in your mouth."

I do not know where you are in life or your walk, but I hope this will encourage and give you hope not to give up or give into the enemy's lies.

When he shared this with me, I could certainly empathize with him. My trials were different, but the pain was just as gut wrenching and the cries to God the same. We will all experience trials in our life and hopefully, from reading this may these become bumps in the road versus a roller coaster ride.

Miracles

Angels of Protection

On June 30, 2015 Ernest Lee Hendrix Jr. was hiking on Green Mountain in Huntsville, AL when he fell 80 feet from a cliff.

When he did not return home, his parents began their search and found his vehicle parked at a Land Trust area. They called 911 and emergency crews joined in to help search for the missing young man. He had been lying at the base for approximately 16 hours.

His mother was the first to locate him lying at the base of the cliff after spotting his backpack. It took responders over 2 hours to carry him up the cliff and get him to the hospital. Reports had indicated that his skull was fractured, slowing down blood flow and oxygen to his brain. "When he fell, he hit the back left side of his head and fractured the skull on his left side. Upon impact, it made his brain bounce in his head, and when that happened, the right side of his brain hit up against his skull, and caused bleeding and swelling." Wilson said. A miracle he was alive. Falling 80 feet and no broken bones?

After several weeks, his family noticed small movements with his right arm and right leg. The family had an appointment to meet with the Shepherd Center in Atlanta, one of the nation's top rehabilitation hospitals for brain and spinal cord injuries. The Athens community and many others, rallied around with prayers and support for Ernest Lee.

Taking one day at a time with many sleepless nights by his family, physical and occupational therapy progressed that Ernest Lee was transferred to the Shepherd Center July 21, 2015.

"Prayer is such a powerful thing and God is so good! Great hearing positive updates." This was just one of many prayers as people followed and supported Ernest Lee and his family. Everyone anxiously awaited daily updates and progress reports.

I remember seeing a special post that read, "Ernest Lee makes everyone smile every day! He is always polite and tells them thank you, when they do anything for him." An amazing young man fighting to overcome many obstacles, yet thinking of others.

July 31, 2015 – "God is so good and faithful! All the glory to God for the continued healing of our Ernest Lee."

When he was in NICU his mom would look at his tattoo and pray to God, "he can do all things through you, so strengthen him God" and Ernest Lee smiled and said "made it here."

August 6, 2015 – Healing and miracles are continuing!

August 9, 2015 – Ernest Lee enjoys his first time outside in the sun. We take so much for granted.

From August 9th to September 9, 2015, he continued fighting through on his therapy and something we cannot even comprehend, to receive his diploma.

He was graduating on to a more intense therapy with different types of drills and occupational therapy, to prepare him for his future of returning home.

On November 5, 2015 Ernest Lee went to see the nurses and staff one last time, he was a graduate!!!! "Thank you to everyone for the letters, pictures, cards, thoughts and mostly prayers. Couldn't have done it without God," said his mother.

November 7, 2015 – Ernest Lee is headed home with his family and new puppy, Cliff.

October 27, 2015 – "God has blessed me with all my progress through my accident and He has blessed me with all of you wonderful people supporting me and praying for me. Thank you all so much!!!!!" says Ernest Lee.

April 18, 2016 – Ernest Lee's mother writes, "Ten months has now passed and Ernest Lee continues on an amazing path of healing and we owe all the glory to God! He has taken steps in his recovery process the medical field says again it had nothing to do with medicine, but by the hand of God. We thank God every day for his continued progress."

Ernest Lee turned 21 on April 23, 2016.

Miracles happen today and Ernest Lee is proof that they do. Despite all the odds, by the grace of an Almighty God, he lives.

"My God sent his angel to shut the lions' mouths so that they would not hurt me, for I have been found innocent in his sight. And I have not wronged you, Your Majesty." Daniel 6:22 (NLT)

Daniel was a man of integrity and work ethic, which made him a target for attack. But, also that he would not turn against God and be faithful in all circumstances. Which caused him to be condemned to the lion's den. Daniel was truly a prayer warrior, believed in it and prayed several times a day. Not only did he pray, but also gave thanks and gratitude to our wonderful Father. Sometimes our lives are so busy that we do not take the time to pray and talk to our heavenly Father, assuming that He will take care of any situation we may have and surely do not give thanks during difficult times.

It was almost as though he was mocked for praying and displaying his service to God. "Your God whom you serve continually, He will deliver you."

Daniel did not begin to pray because his circumstances were challenging, he had made this a habit. The angels protected Daniel while locked with the lions.

"Who through faith conquered kingdoms, administered justice, and gained what was promised, who shut the mouths of lions." Hebrews 11:33 (NIV)

"Beware that you don't look down on any of these little ones, For I tell you that in heaven their angels are always in the presence of my heavenly Father." Matthew 18:10 (NLT)

God placed a safety net underneath Ernest Lee to ease his fall and surrounded him with angels of protection.

Failed to Yield

A miracle as Harold would say. It was a beautiful sunny day and he had decided to get out for a ride on his motorcycle. As he was approaching an intersection, he recalls the Holy Spirit nudging him not to turn in the direction he was considering. He had always followed the same route through the county back roads, but this time wanted to go another way. The nudging was strong, but he ignored it and turned the way that was a no.

He never gave another thought to the ignored prompting and kept riding. He was crossing an intersection, when a car failed to stop. His bike hit the back of the car, shooting the bike off into a transformer box and propelling him through the back window of the car. The impact was so hard that when he went through the window, this drove him directly into the driver breaking the driver's jaw with the helmet. Harold says that if that strap on the helmet had not moved up a little that he would have been decapitated. He sustained thirteen broken bones from his foot to his shoulder, was in a hospital bed for months and not returning to a normal life for a year.

He said there were two things he remembered. One, he should have listened to the Holy Spirit guiding him and trying to protect him. Secondly, he knew there were angels around protecting him or he would not be here today to share his story. He is a miracle to survive and gives God all the glory.

Soft Landing

My daughter had a curfew to be home at 10:00 p.m. because the weather forecast was snow for later that evening and she was going to be about 20 miles from home traveling county back roads. The snow came in earlier, so I had tried calling her to let her know to start home. I never could reach her and had left voice mails, but nothing. After several calls and hours had gone by, then I really began to panic. I contacted the sheriff's department to ask if there had been any reported accidents because that was not at all like her not to answer her phone or be home on time. Finally, I receive a call from a police officer that she was with him. He had been behind her and was worried about her, so he turned the lights on and when he did she swerved and lost control of her car. He tells me that she is lucky to be alive, but she is not injured. The officer had the car towed due to road conditions, so the next day we go to look at the car and I am thinking it would be totaled from the description he had given. Not a scratch on it, nor did the air bags deploy. He said it was though an angel lifted her up and sat the car down gently.

After reading the above stories, my hope is that you believe angels are very real and miracles do happen.

The greatest miracle was Jesus becoming man to take on our sins by dying on the cross. Jesus performed many miracles, but those with little faith did not believe. Miracles happen today, but many go unnoticed because they do not believe. People do not believe that it is God, but a coincidence that someone may be healed from sickness and disease or survive a horrific accident.

"God also testified to it by signs, wonders and various miracles, and by gifts of the Holy Spirit distributed according to his will." Hebrews 2:4 (NIV)

Hearts of Homeless

Hear Me, I Am Not Lazy and Crazy

The next time you go through an intersection and see someone standing holding a sign "will work for food," or "Hungry," they are begging to be heard. If you stop and give someone money, do not worry about what happens when you release that; it is in God's hands. Please do not assume they are using your generosity for drugs. Follow along and hear them as I share a life of living on the streets.

It is true that through your pain you find your purpose and I found my purpose helping the citizens of homelessness. It is amazing how people seem gracious and enthusiastic when you are in a checkout line, until you swipe an EBT card. Their facial expression and tone of voice, says it all.

I became involved through my church as an outreach and I would attend a Wednesday Bible Study at First Stop (which empowers the homeless to a better life), to become involved and get to know them. Every week I learned a little more about those who attended the study and stayed for lunch as they grew to know me. I became a familiar face, which formed great, trusting friendships. After attending for a few months I asked if it would be okay to begin a praise and worship to coincide with the study, so we did. I would arrive at 11:30 a.m. with the music and our choir would gather to rehearse before the service at 12:00. They called themselves the First Stop Choir. Unbelievable talent!

Word spread that we now had music, and more began to join and this went from 5 or 6 in the beginning to 20-25 in attendance. Not everyone would participate and sing along, but they enjoyed the music. As I mentioned previously, do not assume you know a homeless friend's heart because you do not. It takes time to build a friendship with them. They don't trust because they have been mistreated by those not on the streets.

They are not lazy. Some have jobs, but not earning a wage that translates into livable means.

- Most believe homelessness is due to substance abuse. Not true, but yes they may self medicate, due to being exposed to a lifestyle in which they are not accustomed. I would self medicate as well, if I lived in the conditions they do.
- The homeless are not crazy. A small percentage may suffer from mental illness, but living on the streets enhances the illness, which is commonly depression. Again, you would be depressed living on the street. Who wouldn't?
- Most believe that this is the homeless person's fault, that they are living this way. Again, a myth.
- When people believe these myths, they are less likely to want to help.

For some, homelessness is temporary, but not always. It seems to be getting worse and more homeless are not just individuals, but families, left to live on the streets. This can happen to anyone, and many are only a paycheck away from being on the streets, because they do not have a support system. You can be homeless, if you have no means of support and sleeping on someone's sofa. You don't have to be living on the streets. Most of us cannot imagine what that feels like to be abandoned and hopeless.

Being homeless does not define that person; yet society labels them. We are all created by God; each one of us unique. That is the way a homeless person should be treated, unique and supported according to their needs.

Share a smile, treat them with respect and listen. They have a voice wanting to be heard, but unfortunately people do not want to take the time to listen and they are pushed aside, feeling humiliated. It is unfair that our homeless feel uncomfortable and unsafe in a country that has so much to offer. The only difference with them and everyone else, is they do not have a home.

A homeless voice will share that being on the streets means you have a high chance of being beaten, set on fire, sexually abused, harassed and will die alone.

Visiting homeless camps will give you appreciate what you have and things taken for granted. These being a roof over your head, with heat and air, running water for showers and bathrooms, toiletry items that are abundantly supplied, access to food and blessed with safety.

I am terrified of snakes; those close to me know that. When I say terrified, I will hurt someone to get away from a snake. It may sound funny, but it is an overwhelming fear.

The first time I served breakfast in what was known as "tent city," a gentleman told me to watch for snakes. I thought he was joking because they would play pranks on me all the time and think it was hilarious. I did not really give it much thought until he told me again, "Watch for snakes." So I asked him to explain that. He said it is nature. For instance, if we throw an apple core away from the tent, that draws rats and then the snakes to the rats.

I thought I would jump on top of the car when he said that. I was "high stepping." He said, "Ms. Tina what are you doing?" and I told him he could call that my "snake dance."

Their homes are tents placed on wooden pallets so that when it rains, the water doesn't flood their home. Not only that, ant spray is a necessity to circle the perimeter of their tents during the summer months. Their bed isn't a soft mattress, but a sleeping bag placed atop a wooden pallet. Nor do they have the luxury of storm shelters during tornado warnings. Their shelter is under a bridge with God. No air conditioning or fans when it is 95 degrees and only a bonfire from donated wood for heat. How cozy and comfortable does that sound? The relief received during these months is either visiting the library, a shelter or soup kitchen.

During one of the cold winter months I recall one of our homeless friends had built a fire to stay warm. He was sitting in a stadium chair close to the fire and his clothing layered, attempting to stay warm. The warmth was so soothing that he fell asleep in the chair and then toppled over into the fire. He suffered from second and third degree burns, just trying to stay warm and survive. Staying warm almost cost him his life.

We take for granted hearing sirens, alarms on our phones or television to alert us of storms. Homeless may hear sirens, but they have no way of knowing when the storm is approaching. They rely on "C" batteries for the radios to give them updates. Batteries are costly, so collectively, groups will either purchase these or businesses will donate and then they are distributed among the camps.

"Not one person can do everything, but everyone can do something."

Other gifts we enjoy are water for showers, to drink, cook and flush. If and when the homeless have access to showers, that is through a shelter. Operating hours of shelters vary, but most are 8:00 a.m. to 4:00 p.m. Monday through Friday. They receive one shower a day and after Friday, that is it until the doors open Monday morning. Sanitary bathroom facilities are non-existent.

Their drinking water is not from a cold refrigerator. It comes bottled and via donations. During the summer months Gatorade is offered to prevent dehydration. Meals are offered through shelters with breakfast and lunch, but dinner may be on their own, again depending on the shelter they are involved with. We are spoiled to a "drive-through" for a quick meal or convenience stores for treats. That would certainly be a gift for someone to take them out for a meal. Again, I do not know if they would accept the offer because going into restaurants draws attention to them and they already feel rejected.

Safety is another issue. We have alarms on our homes and fencing around the property, they do not. What they may have is a dog. You wonder if they are homeless, living in the woods why would they have a dog. For protection! Many suffer from violence, which you may think this is from other homeless individuals, and sometimes it is, but a lot comes from people taking advantage of their hardships and lack of privacy.

Gene is one of the kindest men I have ever met. It was unsafe for him to be isolated, living in a tent behind an abandoned church, but we could not convince him to relocate and live among others in a camp. We would go every Sunday to visit and as we approached we would call his name and he would slowly crawl out of his tent. There was a picnic table located near his tent and we would sit and talk with him. He would always ask if it would be okay if he read scriptures from the Bible, like a Bible study class for us. After his reading, then he would pray. Why would anyone want to harm a wonderful man like him, but two teenagers did. One night, very late, Gene was sleeping when the teenagers pulled him out of the tent beating him so badly that it broke his jaw, cut his face to the point one of his eyes was swollen shut then left him there helpless. Thank God for an angel watching over him.

On another incident we received a call that he was in the emergency room and thought he was dying. It broke my heart to think that he would die alone, so I left the Manna House (this is for the homeless) and went to sit with him.

When I arrived he was still unconscious. After and hour or so went by, he finally opened his eyes and asked me what I was doing there. I told him to be with him because I cared and was his friend. He began to cry because he said no one would have ever done that for him. We talked for several hours until they released him and I drove him back to his camp.

Engrave this in your heart. As the nurses were preparing the discharge papers, I told him I would get the car and pull it around to pick him up. I parked at the door and went to roll him out in the wheelchair. As I was assisting him to the car, he looked up and said "I am so sorry I smell so badly and I will be getting in your car." That nearly broke my heart. I told him he was fine and not to worry about anything.

We left and went to McDonald's ordering through the "drive-through" because he asked to please not go in. I purchased several items to make sure he had enough to eat for that day and some for the next. He asked if he could eat a little in the car and that was fine with me. But, he didn't eat very much and asked him why, because he had mentioned he was starving. He said that when you are homeless you learn to ration your food and you cannot eat very much at one time, only small portions.

We arrived at his camp and I made sure that he had his food and walked him to his tent. As I turned to walk away, he gave me a hug, thanked me and began to cry. This is what he said as he was crying, "I am so afraid I am going to die alone." My heart felt like it was shattered in a million pieces because I knew I was doing all I could to help him. I gave him a hug and told him that God was watching over him and walked away to my car. The minute I closed the car door, I wasn't just crying, but uncontrollably sobbing. The homeless are so vulnerable and become isolated from society.

Gene became homeless after he lost his granddaughter to cancer. At first he blamed God and went into a state of depression. From the depression, he lost his job then his family and became "un-housed" without a support system. This is one of many that experience homelessness and not due to substance abuse. This is just one of the misconceptions about homelessness.

The homeless became my friends and I wanted to help in a capacity that would change lives. So, I served on the Board for First Stop (empowering the homeless) as a Fundraising Representative. The money raised from the events would assist with individuals and their case to reintegrate them back into society. You cannot take someone that has been alienated and expect them to have control over their life when they have become dependent on others to survive. This takes time and work.

My hope is that the next time you see someone standing out holding a sign, shivering in the cold, hungry and needing help you will remember, they are alive and just like you and I. Everyone has a story.

Shamal and the Gift

Saturday, December 15th was a day that certainly opened my eyes. I was not particularly excited about another day at the gym due to the fact I spend so many hours there already helping others, but God wanted me moving in that direction.

On my way to the gym, I stopped by the bank. To save time, I pulled into the drive-through lane and apparently others were thinking the same thing because all three lanes had at least two or three cars in each lane. As I am waiting for the cars to move, which was taking an unusually long time, my eyes were drawn across the road to Reed Chiropractic Clinic. Normally they are closed on Saturdays, but on this particular day, they were seeing patients. As I watched patients entering the building, I noticed an African American man wearing a camouflage jacket and sitting on a duffle bag to the south side of the building. He appeared to be homeless from what I could see. The longer I waited on the drive-through line to move, the more God began working on my heart to go help this young man. My first thought "I wonder if Dr. Reed knows this man is sitting outside of his business." Then the Holy Spirit prompted me to give this man the $20 I had in my wallet.

Right now you may be asking yourself how I was sure this prompting was of God. With me, it is a feeling I know without a shadow of a doubt. Some may say it is a "gut" feeling. The Holy Spirit communicating with me is just a good clear, inner knowing, like a million butterflies in my stomach. A feeling like I am about to jump out of my skin if I don't act on the prompting.

After completing my bank business, I exited so that I was clear of traffic and could park my car and get the $20 from my wallet. I wanted to have the money in hand and ready when I drove across the road. I had the thought, "Here I go."

I drove across, parked the car and decided to go into Dr. Reed's office to make them aware of the situation, and that I was going to go talk to this young man. Traci Reed, Dr. Reed's wife, was standing in the waiting area. I shared with her about the young man, and she said that Dr. Reed was aware of him and had given him something to eat and drink earlier.

I left to make my way to the end of the building, and as I approached him, I notice he has his head down in his hands with the jacket hood pulled up and just appeared so lost.

Me: "Sir, are you okay?"

Him: "I am hoping a friend comes to get me or a bus comes by. I was at Jack's, but they wouldn't let me stay."

I thought to myself, 'good luck with a bus coming this way. They only stop at the Bus Stop located across town.'

Me: "How long have you been sitting out here?"

Him: "About 20 minutes."

Me: I shake his hand and say "My name is Tina, and yours is?"

Him: "Shamal. Nice to meet you, Tina."

Me: I give him the $20 and told him to be blessed, and may he have a Merry Christmas.

Shamal stood up and began to cry then said: "May I give you a hug?"

I gave him a hug and told him to be careful. He said, "I am going to Mike's Food Mart (which was next door) and get snacks." He did just that, and I got it my car and drove away.

I went on to the gym, and on my way back I decided to go back by and see if Shamal was still there. As I approached the intersection, I was stopped by a red light, but I could see where Shamal would have been sitting. What do you know, I saw a Greyhound bus and Shamal is getting on it.

The WOW factor is that Greyhound buses never drive this road. I was aghast, openly shocked. I even called a friend to share with him what had happened. He reiterated that buses don't take that route, ever. Only God could do this.

I was in awe of the entire morning and replaying this as I drove home. When I approached my driveway, I noticed something on my front porch, pressed up against my front door. I parked my car, got out and I could see that it was a Christmas gift. It had no name, tag nothing to show who had left this. A blessing from God.

Later in the afternoon as I journaled the events of this day an e-mail popped up and it was a devotion by Joseph Prince. At first, I was going to delete it without reading it, but that little nudge prompted me to open it. It read:

Practicing God's Presence

"God has promised you His constant presence but are you conscious of His presence every day? (Hebrews 13) When you are conscious of His presence every day, you will experience a peace that gives you rest, joy, inexpressible in your spirit and a power that nothing in this world can offer."

Confirmation!

I share this with you so you may better understand the Holy Spirit and yield to Him. The Holy Spirit will show you how to discern when it is really Him communicating to you versus when it is your own emotions or imagination talking to you.

2 Corinthians 3:17, Romans 8:16

Shredding the Label

"Special Needs"

God said we are all special. "Before I formed you in the womb I knew you, and before you were born I consecrated you; I appointed you a prophet to the nations." Jeremiah 1:5 (ESV)

Special Needs children in our society today are misunderstood and pushed aside. Some even mistreated because people do not want to invest the time in getting to know them. Sure they may not think or behave like others and have emotional quirks. We all have something unique about us. How do you feel when someone has treated you unfairly or has been disrespectful? Frustrating is it not? When someone struggles intellectually, please do not place them into a stereotype as being "stupid."

I have witnessed the stares and glares from others when a special child may not be acting as deemed, appropriate, in a social setting. The whispers can wreak emotional havoc on a special child. To the point, they internalize this believing everyone hates them.

Get to know them and you will find they are affectionate, fun and innocent. They are not perfect, but neither are we. Do not place high expectations on them and have them perform as if they are robotic. If you do this, with their emotional sensitivity, they may withdraw and suffer anxiety from fear of failure, robbing them of opportunities to lead an ordinary life. The labels are placed as "special needs," and not entitled to participate in what is called "regular/ordinary" activities. They have been segregated, and the effects from experiencing this as a child, carry into adulthood. This limits their dreams and drive, placing a barrier around them that they are at best "marginal" in society.

Think about how parents feel when their child is pushed aside in school. The parent's heart wrenching as they watch their child may be made fun of and then school becomes a chore for them. Parents observe their child watching others receive "Outstanding Achievement" awards when their child is overlooked. The efforts of a special child are seldom acknowledged, even though the parent and child have spent countless hours doing studies when everyone else has completed theirs and moved on. There are adults and other children that treat them as though they have the plague. Having very few friends and rarely being invited to outings such as birthday parties or sleepovers. So they spend time home alone finding ways to entertain themselves trying to mask the pain they feel by being rejected from others. How would you feel if your child were treated this way?

What you speak over someone, is it encouraging and positive, or negative and tearing them down? Giving them a chance not only blesses their lives, but yours as well. Society may let them down, but God will always be there when the world is so cruel.

At seven years old, so many labels and limitations had been placed on this little boy, such as slow, uncoordinated and different. All negative. People had placed him in a box called his "home" because others did not accept him. His mother would include him in activities with his younger brother, but that did not seem to work well. His younger brother was quite talented when it came to sports and activities. This just led to isolation even though they were all together. They would find him sitting or playing alone.

His mother contacted me and asked if I could help him learn to swim. She said others had told her that he would never swim. He could not focus, easily distracted and uncoordinated. After sharing this with me and I had never met him, I too had my doubts.

Not one, but several had told her this; what would make me qualified to break through, teaching him the skills needed to swim? I did not want to waste her time or give her false hope. God placed us together!

I prayed about it and God gave me peace, strength and a positive attitude that I could help him. It would take planning, consistency and patience.

I called the mother to set up our first meeting and to assess my new swimmer. After meeting him, I will be honest, I felt like I was jumping in over my head. But, I knew God had this and we were moving forward.

Special Needs children are usually drawn to the water and drowning incidents are high. They see, feel and experience the water differently, yet it is very therapeutic.

So my new little swimmer, wanted to be close to the water, just not in it.

His sessions would be three days a week and each session, in the beginning, it was about effort and building trust with him. He needed to know that I would protect him and I had confidence, he was going to swim.

The first week was having him sit on the step of the pool, the water barely flowing over his waist. We would sit in the water together and play games. After a week, he was comfortable enough to place his face in the water and blow bubbles. Seems easy doesn't it? This was significant with him. He would practice this at home in the bath tub and he was so proud. This was an adaptive phase being reluctant to take the plunge.

Next, as I held him, we went out into the water, and I would twirl him around and while holding him. He would blow "fish bubbles." Then I would dip him down until the water was chest level. That was little scary for him, and he had such a hold on my neck I had to pry his fingers apart so I could move. Three feet of water is what we consider "wading" level, but not with him. Even though he could touch, you would have thought I was releasing him to drown. So this dipping process took a little longer.

This is when my patience was tested as well. Reminding myself, this was going to take longer and we took each day without expectations. Learning was based on his level.

When he realized I would not abandon him, the water became calming, fun and unlocked many benefits.

A kickboard was now introduced. I would support him, but he was holding onto the board and moving through the water as though he were swimming. Flotation and kicking skills come naturally with most, but with some students it takes consistent effort.

As the anxiety subsided, the next few sessions he took off on his own with the kickboard. I was close by, but he was getting this!

He had mastered the basic skills and ready for stroke technique instruction. As I held him in the water, he did great combining arm and leg movements. The effort this little guy was putting forth was tremendous.

It made me think, here is this sweet, innocent child going after something he truly wanted, which was to swim, and fighting every step of the way. Defying the odds that he was told he could not do this. We on the other hand, have visions of what we want in life, opportunities and doors opened for us and we throw them away. Why, because we fear failure and the unknown.

God wants us to walk by faith and Satan wants us to walk in fear. A child just walks in freedom because most of the time he does not know to be afraid. His mind has not been contaminated with negative thoughts. Those thoughts come from outside forces, called people, and people speaking that over you can keep you frozen in fear. God knew he could accomplish this and placed the right person in his life to guide him. Have you ever wondered how many people have wasted their talents and gifts because they gave way to fear?

My special little guy was moving forward and was swimming. It might have been with me holding him, just like God holds us up, but he was making great strides. His next phase was for me to gradually release my hold and allow him to swim solo. Little by little, I moved my hand and now he was swimming. Sure, there were times he quit kicking and his head went under, but he was no longer frantic in the water. Many of us, if our head went under we would drown. He was continuing to improve on the swimming technique and longer distance. The goal was to swim half the length of the pool, staying close to the wall. I would be walking on the deck, staying close in case I needed to jump in with him, but I had all the confidence he would receive the medal of swimmer. Not only that, this would shred the labels that many had placed in his life.

Test day had arrived. It was a Friday afternoon and he was excited. His mother stood outside a glass door, where she could observe but would not be a distraction. We both were in the water warming up and swimming a little, then he said he was ready. I reassured him that I would be close and if I saw that he needed me, I would jump in. I could see he was anxious, so we got out of the pool and walked down the deck to the starting point, where I lowered him into the water. He was holding on to the wall and I told him when I say "go" start swimming. He swam like a champion all the way to the end. He did it!

All he needed was someone to believe in him, have patience and offer encouragement. A swim with God brought both of us out of the wilderness. He had both of us to himself and wonderful things happened because we are someone in God's eyes.

"Do not let your hearts be troubled. You believe in God; believe also in me." John 14:1 (NIV)

This little boy and his family seemed to be standing on a horizon looking at a bleak future wondering what to do. How many of us have troubled hearts feeling confused, worried or overwhelmed? Delete the negative thoughts and reprogram your mind with "I can do all things through Christ that strengthens me."

> Jesus' disciples felt the very same way. At the age of thirty-three, their Lord is leaving them. The disciples were not expecting this. They were counting on Jesus being around for a very long time. Jesus addresses His disciples' heart trouble with some heart-to-heart words. He says to them and to us: "Believing leads to seeing." www.Bible.org

A Revolving Door

> A revolving door typically consists of three or four doors that hang on a central shaft and rotate around a vertical axis within a cylindrical enclosure. Revolving doors are energy efficient as they prevent drafts (via acting as an air lock) thus preventing increases in the heating or cooling for the building.

We wonder sometimes why it is so challenging with relationships and people in our lives. Some are great and are lasting friendships. When others the minute the door opens they walk right out, but we seem to continue allowing them to walk in and out. We are dizzy from walking in circles. Maybe we pushed one out the door, but something within us said to allow them back in. I have had seasons in my life they turned into great friends and others that were just lessons that opened my eyes. A few that left me scratching my head and perplexed.

So we are in this revolving door and can visually see, but lack of wisdom and discernment as to where they fit. Who we allow in our life is very important, and sometimes we allow those who will trip us up because we are so lonely, we lose focus. Those people jump in and out of these compartments because we allow it. Yes, we do it. We are the ones saying yes or no. If you are single and lonely, you are on the devil's playground. It hurts. Let us look at this:

- Do you have a big heart wanting to help others?
- Do you fall in love quickly and hard?
- Are you encouraging and a people pleaser?

That's the cahracteristic of a caring and sensitive person, but the reality is we open the door allowing anyone to enter. Does that make you a bad person? Absolutely not, it just means that your focus has strayed from God.

Having a big heart, being caring and sensitive, loving and wanting to bless others are wonderful traits and you are uniquely made.

If our eyes are set on God, we would not allow just anyone to enter our lives.

"I will praise You, for I am fearfully and wonderfully made." Psalm 139:14

Begin to pray about who you will allow to enter your life and ask God to close the doors to the ones that will not honor you. You are valuable, Jesus died for you.

Stay in God's word. That doesn't mean skim over the words and think you have it. Walk it out and get your heart right. Do not settle!

Ask yourself this; the person you meet, talk with and are thinking about, will they draw you away from God and pull you into the world? The enemy shows us the glitz and glamour of a relationship, with all the flashy, excitement and fun of the first impression performance. We know, we have seen it and done it. First impressions are enticing, almost blinding. Blinded by the pleasures of the world.

Desperation clouds the truth.

A beautiful girl had met this man and had been talking with him for a couple of weeks. They had shared their spiritual walk, they had similar mornings of coffee and devotional time etc. Conversations are comfortable and they decide to spend some time together on a weekend outing. They go out of town to a beautiful resort, he books two rooms for them (being the gentleman), they play golf together arrive back at the hotel in time to rest a little before leaving for an elegant dinner. He arrives at her door and when she opens the door, his eyes light up and he says "you are stunning!" She replies, "You look so handsome." She takes his arm and they walk toward the elevator. She notices, he is continuing to stare at her and she is feeling like a princess. As they walk by the hotel desk, comments are made about how great they look together. It is like the movie "Pretty Woman." Dinner was romantic, they return back to the hotel with him escorting her to her room and then he leaves for his.

The next morning he brings breakfast to the room and they sit on the hotel balcony admiring the scenery, talking and enjoying their time together.

It is time to checkout and both depart in different directions. They lived 4 hours away and had met at a half way destination. He contacts her to let her know that he has arrived home safely and she had made it home at about the same time. They chatted briefly and then she never heard from him again.

She was totally confused. The reason being, there were compliments all weekend. He was such a gentleman and no indication whatsoever that he was not interested in her. The only thing she could think of was this. God knew something more to this relationship and closed the door. She had prayed about this before ever leaving for the weekend, asking God for her protection and to guide her if he would be good for her life.

When beginning a new relationship, let the the other person know that you are valuable and set your standards, aligning with God's Word. He will prune those people trying to come into your life. See yourself as God sees you and believe you are worthy. Do not compromise your beliefs, this only creates emotional pain.

"Above all else, guard your heart, for everything you do flows from it." Proverbs 4:23 (NIV)

I personally would find what I thought was going good in a relationship and then I might not hear from them again. Sure I felt rejection, but then as I thought about what I had asked God, "Close the door if they are not healthy for me." So in fact God was protecting me.

Remember your life is not a revolving door. Someone who wants to come and go at his or her convenience needs to be a NO.

Set healthy boundaries and keep those in place. The fence is up and not just anyone deserves a place in your life. That is earned.

You can love someone from a distance.

A Wedding To Remember

A couple remembers the details of the wedding from honoring God, to the beauty and seriousness of the wedding and a lifetime together. This particular wedding will always hold special memories, like none other.

Attention was given to all details of the wedding that would take place in October with perfect fall weather. Selecting the invitations, dresses, flowers and décor definitely reflected the colors of fall. Even to the menu selection, which would be foods that normally are served for a southern Thanksgiving meal. The most important decisions were who would walk her down the aisle and who would perform the ceremony. That was easy, the man she adored the most, her grandfather.

Lauren was so close to her grandfather she wanted him to be with her during this special day. She was the first grandchild and he said then he knew why God called them "grand" because they are so special. Isn't that what most grandparents do, spoil the grandchildren? He certainly made an impact on her life. Not always buying her things, but spending quality time with her. Helping her learn to read, to swim, ride a bike, drive a car and sitting next to her in church. This is one example. When she had her driver's permit he allowed her to drive his car. He would pick her up from school and then she would drive to work, with him in the passenger seat as the instructor. They both loved this time together. Certainly he had more patience than I did. So much so, that he took her for the driver's license test. My nerves would have been shot. Speaking of driving, he taught all four grandchildren how to drive and three of the four took their driver's license test in his car. This is something they all looked forward to.

This is how special he was to Lauren. One day he came to visit and he always loved sitting in our 'big mans' chair. So that is where he sat. As we began talking, Lauren had heard us and came in the room to see him. She never said a word, walked over to the chair, sat down and snuggled under his arm. Lauren was 21 years old. I don't know many girls that age that would have done this. That is how much she adored him.

Now you see why the decision was easy as to who would walk her down the aisle. Now, who would perform the ceremony? Lauren's great uncle, who just happened to be her grandfather's brother, was a minister. Her grandfather was so thrilled that she and her fiancé had chosen to have him marry them. A family wedding!

The rehearsal was so much fun watching them together and you could see the excitement in his face knowing he was going to give her away. Something special about this wedding, he was not in good health and was unsteady when walking. He would need assistance getting around. The wedding was taking place outside in a garden area of an antebellum home. The bride would walk across a bridge and her grandfather would be waiting to greet her and escort her down the aisle. Plans were made for how we would get him to the point to meet her and that he wouldn't be too tired while waiting. So we placed a chair at the bridge that he would sit and rest until she walked across. There he would actually take her arm and together, her supporting him, would allow him stability to walk with her. He had just turned 79.

The wedding day arrives, everyone getting dressed, pictures are being made and then it is time for the ceremony to begin. The wedding coordinator gives the cue for the music and we begin. We exit out a side door with my mother, my father in the middle and I am on the other side supporting him. We walk to the front row of seats and my mother stops there to be seated as I continue to walk my father to the edge of the bridge. He sits down and I return to sit along with my mother. The Maid of Honor, which is the bride's sister, makes her way across the bridge, then the flower girls and now the bride looking radiant strolls across to greet her grandfather. I remember the look on his face and it was the same look as he had the first time he laid eyes on her when she was born. He stands when she arrives and they walk arm and arm, making their way to the altar. I have never seen a man so proud, as he was that day. Just beaming!

Beautiful blue eyes with serenity of the sea,
Reflection of the skies on a bright and sunny day,

My little hand in yours, my protector and my guide,
Don't walk too fast, Granddad, for I am by your side…
By Sinead Harris

How special to see his two granddaughters standing at the altar with him and he is so honored that his brother, a Baptist minister, is performing the ceremony. His other brother and two other grandchildren were in attendance as well.

When asked, "Who gives this bride? He replies, "Her family." Not a dry eye then. What a day to remember.

Three months after the wedding, he was diagnosed with cancer. Now we know why he wasn't feeling well. Five months to the day of the wedding, he was escorted home to be with the Lord. Looking back, we were so thankful for the pictures, his strength to give her away and the most incredible wedding. God knew the importance of those memories. We needed each one to help fill the void in our hearts after losing him.

"But the comfort (which is) the Holy Ghost, whom the Father will send in my name, he shall teach you all things, and bring all things to your remembrance, whatsoever I have said unto you." John 14:26 (KJV)

Rebound

We are to rebound into living, not just sitting in the bleachers. Sometimes life beats you down to the point you have no energy to put forth effort in an attempt to rebound. We know that feeling, "it just isn't worth it." The discouragement comes from the enemy and encouragement from God.

Let us break down rebound:

1- Keep your knees soft and bent. This will have you low and blocking. Ready to move.

This is the same with God. Knees bent kneeling and praying for the "right" person or persons in your life. The person or persons equally yoked (two believers sharing the spiritual connection of God), supporting, uplifting and encouraging. We are either following the directions of God or being guided by unbelievers. Unbelievers had no road map of direction and guidance.

2- Keep your hand up and arms open wide allowing wide coverage. If you arms are up, you are prepared to receive His blessings and continuing to praise Him. If you arms are not up, the enemy has the opportunity to pin you down.

Praise Him for removing those that are not healthy in your life with arms up, you then are free to move forward boxing the enemy out.

3- Boxing out is necessary because your feet are planted firmly and standing your ground against the enemy.

Be prepared to reposition if the enemy makes a move. Power forward is a position for the tallest player. You are tall in Christ. Gifted to grab rebounds.

"... and that they will come to their senses and escape from the trap of the devil who has taken them captive to do his will." 2 Timothy 2:26 (NIV)

"... your beginnings will seem humble so prosperous will you future be." Job 8:7 (NIV)

Rebounding positions us for people coming and going from our lives. We are planted in receiving those that God places to help and together both learn. Life is like a puzzle, placing the piece that fits.

If the piece is not a fit, we are still strong in life to release and trust God with the move. We have learned everything we need to know and time to move on. Do not try to hold on to something God has moved. You will be thrown off balance with conflict and chaos.

We are called to follow Jesus, not once, but every day. Life is very much like a puzzle. With lessons that are little pieces, with encouragement, people or our walk along the way. We may see these every day and not even realize the piece was within our reach or then again it may be like a treasure hunt, always searching. Whether we have it within reach or are searching, my hope is that you are seeing the puzzle come together. What will be when the puzzle is complete, the big picture.

Stay planted and work with each piece as it is presented to you. It does take patience and endurance, do not rush God's plan.

Push Not Ride

It is amazing how spoiled we are in our society. Everything seems so convenient and easy. We have microwaves for quick meals, dishwashers to save time, washers, dryers, drive-through car wash and riding mowers which saves a lot of time and effort. No one wants push mow a yard in the sweltering heat, when you can ride. I know, I was spoiled to a riding lawn mower to cut my grass until it burned up. Most take this for granted, like I did until it's time to shop for a new one and experience the sticker shock.

It is a huge deal. I couldn't afford to purchase another riding mower nor did I have the money for a lawn care service. I never thought I would be thankful to have a push mower and walk an acre in the hot sun. Who would be crazy to want to walk it when you could ride?

Several days went by and I didn't know what to do or how I was going to maintain my lawn. I would find myself looking at the yard and crying, like that was going to help. Continuing to pray for answers, I shared this with a friend. I truly was concerned. A few days after sharing this, that same friend called and he had purchased a new push mower for me. To have a mower was such a blessing. It didn't matter whether it was a basic or top the line with all the 'bells and whistles. I had never been so grateful in my life. God had answered my prayers!

I was so excited to have this new gift. It was like Christmas. A blessing not only to walk and do yard work, but this was therapeutic. Getting exercise and clearing my thoughts. The more I pushed this mower, the more thankful I became for the little things in life.

I would find myself thinking each week as I cranked the mower, how blessed I was and how thankful to have a friend that was so thoughtful. After cutting the grass each week, I would wash the mower down and clean it up like it was brand new. My thought was, if God blessed me with this I needed to do the best I could to maintain it. After many miles with this mower, in the middle of cutting the grass one day, it died and would not crank again. I tried everything to get it running and nothing would happen. So I cleaned it up and placed it in the garage. Because I really liked that one and it was affordable, I purchased another just like it.

One day I was purging the house of clutter and decided I was going to place all the items on tables at the end of my drive and allow anyone that wanted them to take and enjoy. There were lamps, artwork, clothes and the push mower that was given as a gift and no longer worked. I had all the items neatly placed and the sign read, "please take anything you like and may you be blessed." I went inside and closed up the house as though I was not home. I didn't want anyone to think I was watching them if they decided to take the items nor feel awkward about doing so. By that evening, all was gone.

About a month goes by and one morning I am in my backyard cutting the grass when I see a gentleman approaching my fence. I stop the mower and walk over to see what he needs. He said, "ma'am I saw your things sitting outside about a month ago and I am the one that took your mower. I was going to break it down and use the parts, but after I began looking at it I realized I could repair it. I thought about your sign and being blessed and in my heart I couldn't keep it. So I repaired your mower and brought it back." I thanked him and told him that I had received such a huge blessing. He said, "No, I am the one that received the blessing."

God surprised me with two blessings!

"God lavished his kindness on us because we belong to Christ."

Ephesians 1:6-8

Think about how you feel surprising someone with a gift and his or her reaction or you receiving an unexpected act of kindness, especially if you ate walking through a difficult time. You see and feel the love placed in this. Not only that, the thought and planning of this surprise. It is like your heart does a flip and you show this from the inside out. If we will do this for others, think about how much God wants to do this for us. He created us and knows every hair on our head.

God is full of generosity and mercy, reminding us frequently with His gifts. Talking about surprises, think about how Mary felt when she learned of her pregnancy and a virgin. That is how He likes to work, unexpectedly.

Remember, to say thank you God because it is never a coincidence.

Blanket of Leaves

Learning to be thankful during a difficult time

It was a cool fall day in November and the front yard covered in a blanket of leaves. I could hardly see any grass, there were so many leaves. You may be thinking how beautiful to see the colors of fall with all the leaves and you would be correct. But, I was going to be spending backbreaking hours raking these beauties. I had procrastinated long enough and it was time. Raking as often as I could was not managing the amount of falling leaves accumulating in my yard from my neighbor's trees. It truly was a blanket covering the lawn. I would rake and think that the yard was neat and within a few days it was covered again. So my thought was to wait and that only made it worse. Mulching the leaves with a mower would have been much easier, but both mowers would not crank on the day that I really needed them. I was discouraged knowing I was going to be spending hours raking and bagging leaves. Raking might not have been so bad, but I was a little nervous with the bending and bagging because I tend to have back issues and this would only aggravate a chronic condition. My thoughts were, 'if you strain your back, you will be out of commission for awhile and unable to work.' I was already allowing negative thoughts to creep in and slow me down.

So I changed into my outside work clothes, put my hat on, went into the garage and gathered my gardening gloves, rake and bags. I thought I was mentally prepared to conquer this task, until I saw all the leaves once again. I just wanted to sit and cry I was so overwhelmed. Sitting down crying wasn't going to get the work done and it was time to 'bite the bullet' sort of speak and just do it. As I began raking and forming piles, it seemed like one foot forward and two steps back with this process because the wind began to blow and was spreading the leaves into the yard. Come on, how many are with me when you think about raking and bagging leaves? It is time consuming and painful.

Thank the good Lord that the wind calmed down enough that I could form leaf piles and they weren't scattered everywhere. After forming many piles, I knew I needed a quick break and allow my back to rest because it was beginning to sting and tighten. Yet, I wanted to press on and get this done. At one point, I just sat down in the grass and began to cry. As the tears were streaming down my face I began thanking God for all He has done for me with the blessings of a nice home and a yard to maintain.

So my pity party needed to end and back to raking. No sooner than I stood up and wiped my tears, my neighbor that lived three houses down, was driving by and stopped. He rolled down his window and said, "Tina, that is going to take you forever to rake all of those leaves." Well, I knew that but not much I could do. I told him that I didn't have a mower to mulch them and this was the only way to clean the yard. He said he would be right back and drove off. I had no idea what he was doing or when he was coming back, so I continued to rake. About 5 minutes later, I looked up to see him driving toward my house on his riding mower. He said, "if it is alright with you, I will mulch your yard." What a blessing. It took him about 10 minutes to go over the yard which would have taken me hours and more than likely ended up with a strained back.

I told him how generous that was and that I could never repay him for volunteering his service. He just looked at me and said that he was glad he came by when he did and was glad to help. In my heart I was saying, 'Thank you God for sending him and at just the right time.'

The Bible teaches us to be filled with joy even during difficult times and show gratitude. I know this is challenging and it has been for me. If you practice and deliberately make choices to think negatively, you will become stressed or you can take captive those thoughts and choose to live trusting God.. When I catch myself going into this mode, I begin talking to God and sharing my feelings with Him. He knows my heart and thoughts, nothing surprises Him. And He does have my best interests at heart. So when tears were streaming down my face doing my yard work, He was not surprised at all. He sent my neighbor to help.

"In everything give thanks: for this is the will of God in Christ Jesus concerning you." 1 Thessalonians 5:18

Think about Job and how he suffered. He lost everything,; his family, home, belongings and health. Even his friends criticized him. But, he never turned against God just continued to praise Him. Jesus was crucified, but he did not complain. Sometimes it is easier to read this than try to wrap your mind around what they endured. We never know until we have walked in someone's shoes.

"Blessed be God even the Father of our Lord Jesus Christ, the Father of mercies, and the God of all comfort; Who comforteth us in all our tribulation, that we may be able to comfort them which are in any trouble, by the comfort where with ourselves are comforted by God."

2 Corinthians 1:3-4 (KJV)

Hearts to Help

The holiday season approaching and definitely in full swing with shopping frenzy, holiday specials, songs on the airways and gift lists being made. All of this was making me rethink Christmas. Where was Christ in Christmas and what about our poor.

The Holy Spirit placed on my heart to reach out to the community and gather gifts for the homeless because they do not experience Christmas time like most families. The gifts would be much-needed items such as coats, socks, clothing, all weather gloves, blankets and toboggans. I was no stranger when it came to working with the homeless. I had accompanied Mike Gordon of the Dream Center, going into the homeless camps on Sunday afternoons. So, I knew their specific needs.

God sure did have a sense of humor. He placed this on my heart December 2, 2016. That meant I had a few weeks to organize this drive, get the word out, begin gathering items and then deliver the gifts to the Huntsville Dream Center (His Compassion Ministries). The organization would then go into the camps and distribute the gifts before Christmas. After thought and prayer, I recruited a dear friend, Karin McAndrew, to assist me in the drive. Together we began sharing our idea with friends. This was not going to be just any charity drive, but one that would make our homeless friends feel special. We asked those donating to please tie a red ribbon around their gift, so when distributed they would experience the spirit of Christmas.

We had two weeks to pull this off. The drive and silent auction would be held December 17, 2016 at the Lions Den Gym in Athens, Alabama. Not only did I want to receive many needed gifts, but also to raise enough money to provide food, tents, batteries, and other items for their survival.

As I was journaling and praying one morning, the amount of $3,000 was on my heart. My hope was the silent auction would bring this amount.

Word quickly spread with help from friends and the local paper, The Athens News Courier. What an outpouring of love. We began receiving bags of the items listed. The ones that did not have a ribbon tied around them, Karin and I would take home, tie the ribbons and place into our marked boxes for the drive.

The day had arrived. Everything set up from silent auction items to apple cider. Boxes filled with blankets, coats, all types of clothing and gift boxes of toiletries filled the entry way of the gym. People began dropping off items at 9:00 a.m. and it was a steady flow until noon. The last silent auction bid was taken and our drive came to an end. The gym was filled with so many gifts for our homeless friends. This was the best Christmas gift I received that year. Christmas is about compassion.

The drive came to a close with approximately $10,000 in value of goods and $500 from the silent auction. I will say I was disappointed with the amount because I was hoping for the $3,000 that was on my heart. Well, $500 for His Compassion Ministries was better than nothing. With this over, I didn't give it another thought nor dwell on the fact I didn't receive the $3,000.

On December 24, 2016, Christmas Eve, I received an e-mail from a gentleman I did not know. He wanted me to share about the Dream Center and working with the homeless. I was wondering how he had my contact information, but I remembered my e-mail was in the news article. Yes, I was skeptical because this was totally unexpected. I forwarded the website and shared what the homeless experience as life on the streets. He responded that he had reviewed the website and made a donation to a ministry that I felt so strongly about.

My thought was, 'I bet you did'. So I wrote him and the e-mail read, "when the Dream Center office opens on December 27, 2016, I will verify your donation to make sure they did in fact receive this and there was not a glitch in the system. May I have your contact information in case of a problem?" After pressing send, I was sure I would not hear from him again.

I hear the sound of an e-mail coming in and it was his response. It read, "maybe this will help." It was an electronic receipt with his name, date, card number, time of transaction and amount.

The amount of the donation was $2,500. You may be thinking that is awesome, just as I did. I was stunned. More importantly, remember the amount that was prayed for, $3,000. The $500 from the silent auction and the gentleman's donation of $2,500 totaled the $3,000. When I had forgotten about it, God shows up with a supernatural blessing. Here I was questioning and doubting the person that God was using to bring forth this blessing.

Do not ever underestimate the power of God.

"For my thoughts are not your thoughts, neither are your ways my ways, declares the Lord. For as the heavens are higher than the earth, so are my ways higher than your ways and my thoughts than your thoughts." Isaiah 55:8-9

Hole-In-One

"Jesus look at them and said, "With man it is impossible, but not with God. For all things are possible with God." Mark 10:27

Some pros and top amateur golfers may have 15 or 20 aces. But average weekend golfers, may accidentally knock the ball from the tee into the hole, despite trying and then they have a huge story and have become a "pro" golfer.

Most that take up golf spend a lot of their time, chasing the little white ball that has veered into the trees. A lifetime of practice and many hours spent to obtain the perfect swing hoping for the hole-in-one. Even the better golfers may come close, but not to drop in. Hit the flagstick and bounce back.

My father was the same way. He played almost every weekend. That I can remember. At the driving range often working on his swing and if he was not playing, he was watching the pro tournaments on television. If he was not home to watch the tournament, he would record it and ask my mom and I not to tell him who won. He loved this sport. So much so, I remember him having an orange ball so that he could see it because there was snow on the ground. A little rain never stopped him.

He would play several courses, but played Monrovia, Municipal and Colonial on a regular basis. At 64 years old and a pick-up game on Monrovia Golf Course would forever change his golf game.

My father's nickname was "Pappy" and everyone knew him by that and he was not just your average golfer. This same year he already had a 71 and two par 72 rounds and a 7 handicapper. At the age of 61, he had a three-under 69 at the Colonial Golf Course.

Over the years my father accumulated many eagles, three shot on par 5s and two shots on par 4s, but never a hole-in-one. It was all about to change.

Rarely, did he play golf alone. This day his golf partner was a long time friend, James Butler. As they warmed up, waiting to tee off, they picked up another gentleman and they would play the front nine as a threesome. My father shot a 38 on the front nine.

Headed for a 135-yard par 3, my father did not have an open path toward the green due to a huge cedar tree blocking the green. A great swing and perfect line, the ball sailed over the top of the tree. One of the men made a comment that it looked good. Well, if you are a golfer looking good and being good is different. You never know until you approach the green and begin searching for your ball. It may have careened in any direction.

My father thought it looked good as well, but when all three approached the green, his ball was nowhere in sight. After searching through the high grass, one of the men suggested looking in the hole. My father walked over and there it was. I remember how excited he was and he had finally done it. How amazing!

He finished the back nine blazing home with a six-under 30. His total for the 18 holes was a 68 and best round of his life.

He had come close several times before when it would look like the ball was going in, but would swirl and come back out. In his mind he never thought this was possible.

Inspired from this, he set his next goal of shooting a 65 at the age of 65. I guess he would leave that to the pros. He would get close like the 68, but never made the 65.

He truly had a story to tell, but he was modest and did not go around bragging about his talent. He knew that God had blessed him with this gift.

He used his gift and knowledge of the game to go on to help many others. I became one of them. I began playing golf with him at the age of 15. His goal for my life was to become a pro golfer and he would be my caddy. I enjoyed golf, but I did not want to devote all of my spare time to the game. I was also involved in other sports. Had I agreed to this, my father would have done anything to make this dream possible.

He was a very patient coach. If you hit a bad shot, he would ask you to tell him what you had done wrong. He wanted you to be aware of your grip, swing, head down and follow through. We were playing golf on a Saturday morning and the busiest time to tee off. I was so nervous, feeling eyes of other golfers piercing through me just waiting for me to make a mistake. Calmly, my father whispered, "don't think about the ones behind you, look forward and focus. Just relax." I closed my eyes, took a deep breath and then looked straight at the ball pulling back smoothly and following through with a powerful swing. As my father would say, "you polled the ball." He was so proud.

Think about what he said, "don't think about the ones behind you, look forward and focus." This applies to all and focusing on our past versus releasing this and moving forward.

"Don't worry about people in your past, there's a reason they didn't make it into your future."

Golf is called a "gentleman's sport," playing the course at an affordable pace being respectful of players in front and behind you. Wave players through if you feel it is necessary to find a ball. Stand quietly and not in the shadow of a fellow golfer, while they are hitting.

"A Gentleman's Game played by a Gentleman known as such because of the Art of Etiquette that grooms a Man."

My father proudly displayed integrity on the course as well as in his every day life. He was playing one day and a few younger men wanted to join him, but they were using profanity. I remember him telling them, that they could play, but that it was not acceptable to use that language around him. He was not rude, no need for it. I guess they wanted to play because it stopped. Set the standard by your actions.

"Walk in wisdom toward outsiders, making the best use of the time. Let your speech always be gracious, seasoned with salt, so that you may know how you ought to answer each person." Colossians 4:5-6 (ESV)

Becoming a successful athlete requires discipline, self-control and developing good habits. This is no different than our spiritual life. Forming good habits of placing God first and asking Him to guide us, the discipline to study and apply His word and self-control when faced with temptations.

An athlete is taught to never give up. God gives us strength through His promises!

"He gives strength to the weary and increases the power of the weak." Isaiah 40:29 (NIV)

We have heard the saying "pick yourself up by the boot straps." Sometimes we cannot find the straps or the strength to pull. When you are feeling weak and down, God will carry you through with encouragement and hope until you can renew your strength. Continue taking steps forward, even if they seem small. Tiny steps become larger steps, then you are off and running.

Believe You Can Do Anything In Christ Who Strengthens You!

Another Blind Side Story

This story began on Wednesday, June 7, 2017, when Nichole Massey at The River of Life church in Huntsville, AL heard the prophetic words spoken over me, and my response into the accuracy of this prayer. Please read 'Powerful Story.'

Sunday, June 11, 2017, I was at River of Life Church and the service was ending when Pastor Jeff Thomas began to speak to a young man sitting at the back of the church and said this, "Linebacker, hold onto Proverbs 3:5-6 and continue your walk with the Lord. God will open doors."

I didn't know 'Linebacker'. Only visiting this church a few times, I didn't know many.

After the service had ended, Linebacker came walking down the aisle and it appeared he was headed straight towards me, so I extended my arm out to give him a hug. I said, "Linebacker, right? Well, you have the opportunity to be a leader with your teammates. Some may walk away, and that stings, but God will work it out. What are your plans?"

His reply, "My goal is to play college football, and maybe I will be lucky enough one day to play in the NFL."

Me, "What is your name?"

Him, "Xavier Hopkins, ma'am."

We talked about the process of being scouted for college ball and that he needed to have film for their review. He shared that he had this available through www.Huddle.com. I asked him if he could give me his contact information and also text me the link to his film because I have friends that are college football coaches and maybe they could offer some assistance. God, was already at work with this young man from orchestrating our meeting to opening doors and aligning those that would guide him. After receiving Xavier's film, I forwarded this to Jacksonville State and my precious friend was blessed with an opportunity, to attend their camp on June 14th. He was so excited, to showcase his talent with other players and have the experience to play in a university stadium. Just one hitch, he wasn't sure that he would have transportation. My heart felt for him, so I volunteered to rearrange my schedule and take him myself. My precious friend, Karin McAndrew, had been witness to this experience, so I recruited her to travel with us. As it turned out, Karin offered to drive, and I would have company during Xavier's camp time.

I don't think the 14th could get here quick enough; he was so excited. The day arrived, Karin and I picked him up, and we headed toward Jacksonville, AL. We arrived, he registered for the camp, had a brief tour of the team film room, stadium and then it was time for him to be dressed and ready to be on the field. Karin and I sat in a balcony area with many others, watching as the drills began. As we watched, many asked this question "which one is your son?" I would point to Xavier, then share that I had met him in church. After the camp ended, Xavier and I met with one of the coaches and asked if there was anything specific he needed to work on. The advice was fine-tuning his skills. We thanked the coach for this opportunity and loaded up to head home. All he could talk about was this experience and said, "I can see myself wearing the red jersey."

A powerful part of this story is that the coach I had contacted was an acquaintance through Facebook. We had never met personally, but he was willing to guide me in helping Xavier pursue his dreams. This coach would come to share that the summer of 2015, while enjoying retirement in Carrabelle, Florida, Pastor Don Carroll of Carrabelle Christian spoke prophetic words over him. These words were that he would come out of retirement and go back into coaching. Not only would he coach, but return to Jacksonville State. He was thinking, 'Why would I do that?' Well, what do you know? It is the summer of 2017; he is coaching and has met this wonderful young man named Xavier Hopkins.

You see in 2015 God was already at work aligning everyone, from the coaches, Xavier, myself and the River of Life Church where we would meet.

Steve Jobs said this:

> You can't connect the dots looking forward, you can only connect them looking backward. So you have to trust that the dots will somehow connect to the future. You have to trust in something – your gut, destiny, life, karma whatever-because believing that the dots will connect down the road will give you the confidence to follow your heart, even when it leads you off the well-worn path. And that will make all the difference.

God was connecting the dots!

Sunday, June 18th, at church Pastor Jeff was actually speaking with a couple about their missionary work in India when it hit me. Xavier will be on his mission field while playing football. Leading others to Christ. Xavier shared this story at church. And his mother shared that when she watched him practice at Jacksonville State with all the players wearing the team red, she could see the blood that was shed by Christ for us. Xavier's stepfather, James Massey, thanked me for being a part of his life and went on to say "this is another Blind Side story."

Xavier went on to have a great Junior and Senior year at Sparkman High School, and I was there cheering him on only missing three of his games. God continued to open doors even after the ending of football season, with an opportunity to showcase his football skills at the Blue-Grey All American Bowl in Houston, Texas. What an honor for this young man.

Celebrating high school football might not seem meaningful to most, but it was for us. I had a Friday night routine of arriving at the stadium early to watch Xavier warm up and also for him to know that I would be in the stands as his biggest fan. As the games would draw close to the end of the 4th quarter, I would make my way out of the stands to the gate where the team would exit the field. As they came off of the field making their way to the Field House, I would watch for Xavier so that I could give him a congratulatory hug. After all the players had made their way through I would go and wait at the Field House for Xavier to change and then we would talk about the game. Creating special memories.

Football season ended, and I felt so lost without watching his games, but as I began to reflect on our journey, this is what God placed on my heart. When we met both of us had only visited The River of Life Church for two weeks. Not a coincidence, this was a God-incidence. Yes, we bonded with a mutual love of football, but it became deeper than this. Xavier was maturing spiritually, and I was watching this unfold. He was steady in his walk when his friends were dating, going to dances, etc. and Xavier was waiting for God to place that special girl in his life. This wasn't easy for him, and he shared this many times how his heart would hurt because he wasn't experiencing high school fun times like most. The waiting paid off, and he met that special girl.

I will never forget in the wee hours of the morning, I heard my phone buzz, and it was Xavier. When I answered, I heard this pitiful voice share that his best friend had been shot outside of a basketball game. His friend just happened to be in the wrong place and the wrong time, when a stray bullet pierced his body. His friend passed away later that morning. My heart was breaking for him having to experience such tragedy at a young age. Through this unfortunate incident, Xavier would dedicate each football game to his friend.

Xavier and I have shared highs and lows, prayers, and walking, not just talking as believers. He shared one night on the phone. "Ms. Tina, I am not sure exactly what to call you when I tell others about you. You aren't my mom, but I feel like you are always there for me, so if it is okay, I will call you my God Mother." Be still my heart.

As you read this story, Xavier will be graduating high school and moving into the next chapter of his life. My hope and prayer is that I will be around to experience what God has for him.

Good Samaritans

This story began the morning of Thursday, July 13, 2017. This day temperatures would rise to 95° and heat index of 100. Very hot and humid in the south.

This particular morning I was truly struggling with hardships of life and as I was preparing to go see a client, I just broke down in tears. Crying and calling out to God. This was not such a sweet talk like most would think. It was a pouring out of my heart and my aggravations with Him. After sobbing uncontrollably for several minutes, I pulled myself together, wiped my face and headed out the door.

As I mentioned, it was 95° and very humid at 10:50 a.m. As I was driving and only about a half mile from my friend's home, I could see something large under a tree. As I got closer, I saw a tall black man begin to sit up. In my heart I knew something wasn't right. He was under the tree and sitting down. I went on to my friend's house because she wasn't far and I knew she would help me.

When I arrived, I began to tell her the story about seeing him. She asked me if he was a large man because she had seen him pass by her home around 10:30 a.m. I told her that was him. As I began soaking a towel in cold water, Sue (my friend) was gathering water bottles and by the grace of God, there was a bottle of Gatorade. Sue began to share that the message in her church on Sunday, July 9th, was Matthew 10:42 "And whoever shall give to drink to one of these little ones a cup of cold water only in the name of a disciple, truly I say to you, he shall in no wise lose his reward." Then we got in the car and headed out to find this gentleman.

As we traveled down the road, he was no longer under the tree. We decided to keep driving to see if he had managed to walk on. He had, we found him. We pulled into a driveway and parked the car.

Me: "Sir, do you have any water?"

Gentleman: "No. You must be Christians. No one would stop to help me. Are you Christians?"

Me: "Yes Sir we are. Sir, here is Gatorade and water. Also, place this wet towel around your neck and cool off. Where are you going?"

Gentleman: "I had dropped my car off for repair and didn't want to inconvenience my wife, so I am walking home."

Me: "Sir, what is your name?"

Gentleman: "William Robinson. Thank you so much for stopping to help me, you don't know how much I appreciate this."

Me: "Mr. Robinson, may we take you to your home?"

Mr. Robinson: "No, I will be okay with the water and Gatorade. I will rest under trees when I need to. Are you born again Christians?"

Sue and I: "Yes Sir, we are."

Mr. Robinson: "God bless you for stopping. You know the message in my church on Sunday was Matthew 10:42, about giving a cold cup of water."

Coincidence that Sue and Mr. Robinson both gave the same scripture? No, a God Incidence!

You see, Mr. Robinson had already walked at least 3 miles and had another 1.5 miles to go, but would not accept a ride. Sue and I got back in the car and left, but I wasn't feeling good about leaving him. I asked Sue to drive to a friend's home, Wade Pepper, in hopes that if a man went to help Mr. Robinson, he would accept the offer. Wade wasn't home, but his son Grant was there. I explained the situation and Grant offered to go check on him in hopes that he could carry him home.

Grant found him walking, pulled his truck close and asked Mr. Robinson if he could take him home. Mr. Robinson accepted the offer. As he began to step close to the truck, he collapsed in the middle of the road. Grant, being a tall man himself, was able to get Mr. Robinson in the truck and cool him off. Grant then drove him home.

He asked Mr. Robinson, "My friends offered to take you home, why wouldn't you accept the ride?"

Mr. Robinson said, "My wife would be upset."

I was sharing this story with a friend and he told me, "There is more to this story, wait and see."

Still concerned about Mr. Robinson. On Friday, the following day, I decided I would go by his home and check on him. I had taken one of my pieces of Canvas Cross Art, placed 7-13-17 on the back along with Matthew 10:42, so that Mr. Robinson would have it to always remember this day. I drove to his home, but he was not there. I left the gift along with a note in his mailbox.

Mr. Robinson called on Saturday, July 15th and we had a wonderful conversation. He told me he didn't realize that he was so dehydrated when we stopped to help him. He thought the Gatorade and water, would hydrate him enough to complete the walk, only to find he was extremely weak. He asked if I had sent the man to drive him home. I told him, I had. I told him the entire story from when I had been crying, to stopping to help him.

Mr. Robinson then said, "I have been a pastor most of my life. Tina, God was showing you He was with you and by both of us sharing Matthew 10:42. God also knew I was in trouble and sent you to help me. I was not wise with the decision to walk in the heat and probably would have passed out and died, had you not stopped. The cross you gave me will always be a blessing of that day. I will place this in my office, so that I may be reminded how special that day turned out to be. I want you to stay in touch with me and please feel free to come by and visit, any time."

This story touched many lives. Not only mine, but my friend Sue, Grant that drove to get him and Pastor William Robinson.

Luke 10:25-37

Powerful Story

On May 31, 2017 this e-mail was written to Steve Spillman.

Subject: Holy Spirit

"I know I am stepping out, but I am saying this. This was on my heart last week and continues very strongly. I believe there is going to come, one more Powerful story for the book."

I was invited to River of Life Church on Wednesday, June 7, 2017. I was really tired and could easily have stayed home, but decided to go. I didn't know much about the church, other than what my friends had shared, and those were complimentary.

The service was very sensitive to the Holy Spirit, moving and not based on time restraints. It was nearing 8:00 p.m. and Pastor Jeff Thomas asked everyone to stand, as he was preparing to close the service. The congregation was standing and in prayer, then he said that everyone remain sensitive to the Holy Spirit and sit quietly continuing in prayer. Several minutes went by and he closed. When he did, he looked at me and said "Will you please come forward and allow me to pray over you?" I wasn't sure if he was speaking to me, he assured me he was. He also asked my friends, Karin McAndrew and Cecilia Joseph if they would come and stand with me also.

Keep in mind, I have never been to this church; I didn't know Pastor Jeff nor did he know me.

As he began to pray over me, others came forward to stand in agreement.

Pastor Jeff began by saying, "I can see a light around you, a glow. You take care of others, reaching those less fortunate and making a difference, when you are doing without. The enemy has been circling you for some time, trying to take you out. That is broken and defeated!"

You may be thinking well anyone could say those things. You would be right. However, on May 10th, Cecilia was at the gym when she looked at me and said "Do you pray?"

Me: "Yes."

Cecilia: "Please pray Psalm 91; you are under attack. Pray this protection, something is not right and I can feel it." I could see goose bumps pop up on her. Goosebumps or sensations are known to be signs of angels. She went on to ask if she could go pray over my home. Fine with me. Again, she had an uneasy feeling then the goose bumps appeared again. Later, I would find out that she could see angels on my roof with stern faces, protecting my home. I knew I was under attack, I had been feeling that myself. Coincidence? Not at all.

Lets continue…

Pastor Jeff continues saying "You have creative gifts and God is going to use those to touch lives, begin businesses and open doors."

WOW! I have canvas cross art in different boutiques/gift shops. On this particular day, I took a chance on a gift shop that had only seen photos of my work. The owner looked over the eight pieces of art. Fell in love with the creative style and decided to carry these in her shop. Well, what do you know. Karin and Cecilia were witness to this step of faith.

Jeff continues with "You have had a ministry stolen from you and God is restoring this." OMG! When I was in my 40's, I had taught Sunday school for many years. Unexpectedly, this was turned over to someone else and without explanation.

As he is speaking, all of these things over me, he takes oil and drops this on my head, anointing me. Then speaks "The cloud is lifted. The darkness you have felt is gone. Someone close to you has stolen what is not rightfully theirs and your family has been torn apart. You are not only going to receive what has been taken, but God is blessing you sevenfold and your family will be restored."

In February 2017, my mother passed away. My spirit, even when my mother was ill, told me something was wrong but I never expected what would come in the days following her death. I was asked not to enter my parent's home. I am the only surviving child and I am not allowed in a home my father worked hard to build and maintain. The person asking this was not a blood relative.

Then I was devastated to find my mother had changed the will and completely removed her blood line from any inheritance. All of her grandchildren and myself, were as though we didn't exist. The way this was handled, actions and words spoken to me were evil.

"The thief who is caught must restore sevenfold." Proverbs 6:30, 31

"Satan is the thief. When we catch him, he will be required to restore seven times as much as what he stole from us." says Creflo Dollar.

Jeff, "God is going to work in your daughter's life." He closes with this, "You have cried many nights and are exhausted. God is lifting you out now, opening doors, prospering you and moving you." This was so true. I had cried so much and was so exhausted. I was ready to give up.

A lady came forward and said "I can see concrete blocks on your feet." That is exactly how I had felt for several weeks. Feeling very heavy and sinking in despair. Again, the enemy circling. I knew exactly what she meant. However, at lunch this same day I was explaining to Cecilia the lyrics of the song Happy Dance by MercyMe. My Living Life Motivational video was a dance to this song demonstrating the heaviness of our hearts and breaking the chains to move.

A gentleman that was seated in front of me during the service approached me and said "As the oil dropped to your head, I could see a hand combing through your hair. Comfort." What came to my mind, was a father stroking a child's hair to comfort and soothe.

I was looking for Karin so that we could leave, and all of a sudden it hit me like a ton of bricks. Tonight was my Powerful Story that I had professed on May 31st. Sharing this with Karin, she looked at me and said "You are right. In the car today, I told Cecilia you would have your powerful story for the book from the service." Amen!

You are reading this story and book, not by chance. Maybe you are a believer, just curious, or riding the fence. May this touch your life in a special way because nothing is coincidence.

Dr. Bill Hamon defined prophecy as:

> ...simply God communicating His thoughts and intents to mankind. When a true prophecy is given the Holy Spirit inspires someone to communicate God's pure and exact words to the individual or group for whom they are intended. It is delivered without any additions or subtractions by the one speaking.

"Do not scoff at prophecies but test everything that is said. Hold on to what is good." 1 Thessalonians 5:19-21

"If a personal prophecy is not of God, the born again Christian will get what is known as a "check" in their spirit-an uncomfortable feeling in the pit of the stomach telling them that something is not right."

The Passport

"The heart of man plans his way, but the Lord establishes his steps." Proverbs 16:9 (ESV)

It all began Wednesday, October 4, 2017. About 1:24 p.m. I received an e-mail from my modeling agency asking if I was interested in modeling overseas. If so, I needed to let them know if I had a passport or would be applying for one. They could not submit me for work until passport ready.

I was hesitant because I never travel to destinations requiring a passport. Maybe this wasn't something I was interested in investing time and money. My personality is to have everything in-line before saying yes.

About five minutes after this e-mail, I heard a car in the drive. I looked out, it is my mail carrier. She had left a package on the front porch. I open the door to see a box, and what do you know, it is from Australia. Coincidence? Never a coincidence with God.

The next day, I am at the gym working out with a long time friend and I am sharing this story. She tells me that she has known me for so long and I have always been one to say NO, if everything wasn't aligned. That I should go for it and get the passport. Why not step out in faith and take a risk. I knew she was right, just hard to admit it.

When I got home from the gym, I picked up the book I had been reading, *Unshakeable Trust* by Joyce Meyer, opening to the place I left off. Low and behold, it read just as my friend shared. Taking a step of faith is a risk. Not knowing what awaits you. Well okay then, maybe I will get my passport and give this a try.

Monday, October 9th, my friend and I are back at the gym and talking about the passport when a gentleman that we both know, came up and said "Would you be interested in going on a mission trip? We leave in three weeks and all you need is your passport?"

My friend and I looked at each other, and then I knew it was meant for me to go. We shared with the gentleman about the previous week and the passport story. He said, "Well get your application in and lets go."

Friday, October 20th the passport arrived!

Sunday at church, The River of Life, Pastor Jeff Thomas asked if anyone would like prayer to please come forward. The tugging of my heart was so strong because I wanted covering before this trip. I made my way to the front where Pastor Jeff led the prayer. At one point he paused, and another gentleman began praying. Pastor Jeff spoke prophetically of the healing that would be seen, drug cartels stopped and turned away, and lives saved.

At the end of the prayer a lady was holding my hands and she said "I see an adult man. He is handicapped in some capacity and I see you working with him. Making a difference in his life."

WOW! I had not shared this trip with my church and there was no way that she would have known about the handicapped gentleman other than God placing this in her heart. I had already seen pictures of the two families we would be building homes for, and yes there was a handicapped man in one of the photos. This is just another confirmation that this trip was meant to be.

This mission trip is a true step of faith for me. Financially, trusting God to provide and take care of all my needs. And the risks of going into Reynosa, Mexico. If you Google Reynosa, as I did, then you might just rethink your plans. Yes, it is an 'Alert' to anyone traveling across the border due to drug cartels.

Here we go, today Saturday, October 28th, is travel day. It is like Christmas, excitement to see God at work! Travel along with me and experience this journey.

Most of the travel day, was just that. After arriving in Texas, we stopped for supplies, then on to purchase groceries before the drive into Reynosa.

What an eye opener as to the way they live. Very primitive in the area we were working. Yet, the people seem so happy with simplicity. Dirt roads, trash thrown on the side in mounds, and most live in shacks. If they are fortunate, they may have a house with concrete floors, walls and roof. No running water, and few have electricity. Words truly do not describe their living conditions.

Well, it is Sunday, Fun Day before our work week begins. Our group is going into Progresa, Mexico for a day of shopping and lunch. We arrive and most have paired up or maybe three to a group for shopping. At one point I am with Sanders Woodroof and David McKenzie. We stop for Sanders to purchase gifts, when I looked across the street to see a gentleman without legs and in a wheelchair. I knew I needed to go speak with him. David said he would go with me, but he would stand away so that I may talk to him.

Remember, the prophetic word spoken from River of Life? So we make our way across the street and David stays a few feet behind. I shake the man's hand and notice he has a bucket in his lap with coins. I am sure people passing by are giving him money. He looks up at me and says "Jesus said you would come." Well, I lost it then. I began to cry and hugged his neck telling him that I did come and Jesus loved him. There wasn't much I could do for him, other than show love. I hugged him once more before David and I walked away. I was a mess. Coincidence? Only God!

David and I met back up with Sanders then David went on to join the others for lunch. As I was waiting with Sanders for key rings to be made, I turned and saw a young Hispanic lady sitting atop a table. Those heart strings were pulling to give her a hug. So, I leaned over, hugged her and smiled. She just kept looking at me, so I gave her another hug. This time she held me so tight. After the beautiful hug, I turned to ask Sanders a question when I felt a tap on my arm. It was this precious young lady giving me five beaded bracelets she had made. My heart was a puddle of goo. Not only did this act of love and kindness touch me, it got to Sanders as well. He opened his wallet and gave her a very nice love offering. When he did, she rubbed her tummy to show she was pregnant. Do you think God was moving? Absolutely!

Sanders made the comment, "If these type things continue to happen, I will be broke." I couldn't help but laugh.

Monday was spent pouring concrete slabs for two homes and also making rebar. My body is surely rebelling at this point. Hard work doesn't even come close to describing this. We have a team (Hispanic friends) through Faith Ministries, that are working alongside of us and actually they are our direction.

This will give you a better idea of a typical day. We get up about 5:00 a.m. have breakfast, get everything prepared for the day, our devotion and prayer time, then about 7:30 a.m. off to the work site. About noon we meet at the church compound and have lunch. After lunch, Hispanic friends and the mission teams have a brief church service together before heading back out for the afternoon. This time has been so special for everyone involved and I have met wonderful friends. Today especially, with triplets named Perla, Rosa and Sonta. Perla and I really hit it off. Joking around with a signature handshake that is our very own. When we were leaving the site today, Perla looked at me and did a lasso move and went "Yee Haw." She was so funny. We may speak a different language, but we both love in a big way.

Tuesday was October 31st and Halloween. As I sat on the second floor balcony, overlooking the dirt roads and shacks, children would come by and want candy. One boy had a Halloween mask on and wanted his picture taken. He was so excited after I had him pose and snapped the shot. Children want to enjoy Halloween/Fall Festivals and it doesn't matter geographically where they are located. God's perfect timing, that myself and a mission trip friend, Judy Rew, could make their night special with candy and fun flashlights.

On Wednesday, after working a long day, we cleaned up and drove into the city of Reynosa for items needed to host a Festival for the less fortunate. When we say Festival, this is cooking hamburgers, macaroni and cheese etc. for about 200 people. The children will receive toys and also the breaking of a Piñata. An exciting time for our Hispanic friends.

Most have heard and seen on the news about the drug wars and cartels in Mexico, but like myself, nothing more than hearing. I will have to say I was naïve to this. As our mission team was driving into the city, the Mexican army's presence is very real. Soldiers standing armed atop armored trucks traveling the roads. Very eye-opening for someone from Athens, Alabama.

We arrive at H-E-B, a large supermarket, and everyone is paired with another team member and given their list of items to shop for. Off we go! Judy Rew is my partner and we finish fairly quickly, so we decide to look around at gift shops located at the front of the store while waiting for the others. Slowly, everyone is making their way to the front.

As Judy and I are waiting, a very well dressed, handsome Hispanic gentleman walks up to me and asks "Where are you from?"

Me: "Athens, Alabama. Are you from Reynosa?"

Him: "I lived in McAllen, Texas for almost forty years but things happen and I am back here now. So, why are you in Reynosa?"

His look was one of peace, certainly not of a bitterness, and he never displayed that in any way.

Me: "We are on a mission trip to build houses for two families in Reynosa."

Him: "How special. What a great heart."

At this time our group is ready to leave and we are moving to the door. He walks along side me, as we continue talking. He shook my hand and said, "Remember Matthew 23:8." I thanked him and we left.

When we arrived back at our compound, I researched this. "But you are not to be called 'Rabbi', for you have one teacher and you are all brothers." Matthew 23:8. (NIV)

This is from Global Church of the Eternal God:

> The passage addresses the danger of becoming proud by accepting lofty and inappropriate religious titles. Christ emphasized the fact that even though He bestowed on His ministry certain functions and responsibilities toward "feeding the flock, the ministers are to understand that they are not in any way 'better' than others. It is God who has given them such responsibilities, that they don't deserve to such functions and that they are 'nothing' in comparison with God the Father and Jesus Christ.

As I thought about this, even though we were in Reynosa as a servant, we are all children of God. The teams ALL worked together to build these houses. That is just it. We were a TEAM.

God does work in mysterious ways and that gentleman could have walked up to any one of our mission team that was in H-E-B and gave that scripture.

God has specific places for us to be at certain times to guide and direct us when He is ready. We should trust Him. He has a purpose where He plants us. May be a short time or long time, but there is purpose. He never makes mistakes. You are where you need to be for a reason.

"Do not be conformed to this world, but be transformed by the renewal of your mind, that by testing you may discern what is the will of God what is good and acceptable and perfect." Romans 12:2 (ESV)

Thank you Athens FUMC and especially Bill Dunnavant for the opportunity to serve with the mission team in Reynosa, Mexico.

What a mighty God we serve.

A Break As A Rest

Where God was leading and what he was showing me, when I conceded in taking a break from life draining things.

My emotional tank was at its limit. Feeling like I was giving to everyone, but denying myself. As I would say to others, "How is that working for you?"

Not very well. I was needing to get away, quiet time with God to replenish spiritually, emotionally and physically. The battle in my mind 'you cannot financially afford to take a break.' Yet if I didn't, I was well on my way to burn out.'

Then I would be of no use to anyone. Jesus took refreshing breaks, so could I.

"Come with me by yourselves to a quiet place and get some rest." Mark 6:31 NIV

Relying on God and exercising my faith in His provision during my time to refresh. My time away from work, social media, e-mails, and friends was just that. Time away to be quiet.

"Teach us to number our days, that we may gain a heart of wisdom." Psalm 90:12 NIV

Even though physically and mentally, I was resting, God was restoring my soul. He was showing me messages for my Living Life Motivational page as well as videos.

An example: I recorded a video on 'Words Are Life or Death' then the

Holy Spirit provided the message and video to follow this, 'Effects of Our Words.' Not only did I receive one message to record as a video, but also four more would follow. He was slowly filling my tank, which had become depleted. With that said, I was open and could see the Holy Spirit giving me inspiration.

An afternoon relaxing on the beach, enjoying the beautiful white sand, sound of the waves and the magnificence of God's creation. The ocean that covers so much of the earth's surface, which can be gentle enough to wade through or powerful enough to destroy. Yet, this ocean would give birth to oil rigs.

Which had me thinking, as I gazed at many placed in the Gulf. Some days being on the beach I could see these so clearly and other days the haze would reduce visibility so that the rigs were a blur.

Isn't that how we see God in our lives? Sometimes He seems so close and clear, when other times so distant. Even though the Lord has touched your life, your vision or perspective is cloudy. Maybe, discouragement, disobedience, bitterness or falling into the world has skewed your vision. A coincidence that God would provide this message? Absolutely not. You see, the Holy Spirit wants the believers and unbelievers to know Jesus.

As I was sharing the messages with a friend, one clearly came to mind. Are our lives like a fountain or river, flowing to reach others?

As I was writing this, a friend was saying that he happened upon a website that gave meaning of people's names. Curious, I asked him to search Tina and tell me what my name meant. He looked at me and said, "You are not going to believe this. Your name means 'river."

Not that I am going to 'hang my hat' on everything from an internet site, but I considered this a confirmation from God. God was again showing himself to me because I believed and I was open to his guidance.

When you feel like your life is like stuffing a glove, take a break so that you can refresh your mind and soul. The Holy Spirit wants to guide both believers and unbelievers. His job is to teach us the truth. He will guide you, if you allow him to. (John 16:12)

During the days of Jesus, the people didn't have cell phones with voice recorders or to film nor did they have pen and paper to write with. They had the truth of the Holy Spirit. The inspiration provided and the revelation. He shines the light so that we may see.

Wouldn't you like to know the plans God has for your life? Get to know God through his word and allow him to lead you. (John 16:13-15)

I received this from a friend and when I asked about it, he said it was on his heart to send. He didn't know why, but thought I needed it. I responded with, "It is God." He said, "It sure is!"

Biscuits

One Sunday morning at a small southern church, the new pastor called on one of his older deacons to lead in the opening prayer. The deacon stood up, bowed his head and said, "Lord, I hate buttermilk."

The pastor opened one eye and wondered where this was going. The deacon continued, "Lord, I hate lard." Now the pastor was totally perplexed. The deacon continued, "Lord, I ain't too crazy about plain flour, but after you mix 'em all together and bake 'em in a hot oven, I just love biscuits."

"Lord help us to realize when life gets hard, when things come up that we don't like, whenever we don't understand what You are doing, that we need to wait and see what You are making. After you get through mixing and baking, it'll probably be something even better than biscuits.

Amen.

Romans 8:28 (NIV)

"And we know that in all things God works for the good of those who love him, who have been called according to his purpose."

Counseling Service

Many occupations such as hair stylists, nailtechs, physicians, dentists, personal trainers, etc. where there is "one on one" time, you tend to hear about health, careers, relationships, and other issues from people you see on a regular basis. The reason is, they feel safe and free to express their life situations in an understanding and encouraging environment. People in general, are emotional. We ride the ups and downs of feeling happy, sad, angry and scared, but the enemy wants us to feel overwhelmed with negative emotions. As the world becomes more complex and everyday life is filled with challenges, you will either be energized or exhausted.

The only professions licensed to counsel are clinical psychologists, counseling psychologists and psychiatrists. "Sigmund Freud opened his private practice in 1886 and Lightner Witmer opened one of the psychological clinics a short time later, in 1896." Our true source for counseling is the wonderful Jesus Christ.

"For to us a child is born, to us a son is given; and the government shall be upon his shoulder and his name shall be called Wonderful Counselor Mighty God, Everlasting Father Prince of Peace." Isaiah 9:6 (NIV)

His title is no different today than it was then and very deserving. He is not angry, and accompanies us through our trials if we allow Him to do so. The Hebrew meaning of "wonderful" is miracle. So He is a miraculous Counselor and can do what no human can. With this being said, why would you want any other guiding than His supernatural insight. The term "counselor' is a secular reference and the idea of listening.

These days we all seem to be the counselors because we share and/or hear daily frustrations, with others. But, are we serving others, or waiting for others to serve us? How are we responding when others are walking through tough times and all they can see are storm clouds in their life?

Are we encouraging them, that these will not last forever and worry only worsens the mood or sharing their band wagon of bad attitude?

"When the devil had finished all this tempting, he left him until an opportune time." Luke 4:13 (NIV)

If we can just remember that the enemy may attack if we are trying to move forward, a breakthrough or doing good to reach others. But, we forget during the trials because we become paralyzed with fear and fall into self pity only thinking of ourselves. If we cannot change the outcome, why waste the energy? We get impatient and want immediate results. I know all too well because I have been the same way; but I am learning to walk this out and wait on God's timing. I did not say it was always easy, it is sometimes minutes or hours at a time to get through a day. If you do not learn to wait, frustration builds then all you do is spew venom. I wish I could turn back years when I would be hysterical and would "vomit" my life on anyone that would listen. My emotions would be running wild and the more I focused on them, the wilder they became. But, you have to believe that you can control your thoughts and this takes practice, like anything else.

Your energy will change if you take the time to begin your day with the Lord before your mind becomes busy. If you hit the snooze button several times, you are well on your way to a stressful day because now you are rushed and behind.

Amazing. If it were a day of shopping, golf, sporting activity, vacation etc. we would not have trouble getting out of the bed a little earlier, we would be eager.

> I have told you these things, so that in Me you may have (perfect) peace and confidence. In the world you have tribulation and trials and distress and frustration; but be of good cheer (take courage; be confident, certain, undaunted)! For I have overcome the world. (I have deprived it of power to harm you and have conquered it for you). John 16:33

If you find yourself in a counseling seat try this:

1. We are called to serve and this may be listening to someone. To be humble and take the focus off of ourselves no matter what we are going through and help someone else. You may end up being

the one blessed, not the receiver.

If Jesus can wash dirty feet and die on a dirty cross, who are we to say we are too good to serve.

2. "You know that I have not hesitated to preach anything that would be helpful to you but have taught you publicly and from house to house." Acts 20:20 (NIV)

Wait for the appropriate time to speak God's truth in guiding and comforting those that are hurting. It may not always be received well, but God will do a work on the one receiving the truth. Keep Him as your center.

3. If God's word tells you something, believe it and do not allow anything to distract you.

We reach people in the work place by exposing them to the light. The light of peace and joy as "Life as a Sermon."

Israel Houghton Lyrics

"The Power of One (Change the World)"

What if it all depended on me
To change the world, to change the world?
What if my only responsibility was
To change the world, change the world?
Let me be the one to start a revolution
Let me sing my song to the people of the world
It all begins with one, the power of one
Joining the hundreds of millions of people believing
In one, the power of one
Don't hang around, stand up or sit down and believe
We can change the world together
We can change the world together
What kind of love can conquer disease?
And change the world, change the world?

What I can do to make poverty history
And change the world, change the world?
Let me be the one to start a revolution
Let me sing my song to the people of the world
To the children of the world
It all begins with one, the power of one
Joining the hundreds of millions of people believing
In one, the power of one
Don't hang around, stand up or sit down and believe
We can change the world together
We can change the world together
Please don't close you eyes, please don't turn away
Let your voices rise, put love on display
And make a difference now
I believe you and me can make a difference now
It all begins with one, the power of one
Joining the hundreds of millions of people believing
In one, the power of one
Don't hang around, stand up or sit down and believe
We can change the world together
We can change the world together
We can change the world together
It all begins with one
It all begins with one
You and me can make it, you and me can make it
You and me can make it better together
You and me can make it, you and me can make it
You and me can make it better together with one.

The power of one doesn't accidently happen, God orchestrates the meeting and gets us together. But, if want to have an impact on others we must be positive and kind. You must not come unhinged when they do not act on what you say. How many times have you offered advice to someone when they are going through difficult times, only to see that they disregarded this and returned back to same patterns? You get irritated and frustrated because they did not respond like you thought they would.

Remember, when you are trying to help someone first did they ask for your advice or did you jump in and try to "fix" the problem? Treat them as you would like to be treated, which may be just listening and making them feel special.

"Do not be deceived: God cannot be mocked. A man reaps what he sows." Galatians 6:7 (NIV)

We are not responsible for changing others. That is God's responsibility and God can change anyone.

It Is God

God the Father , God the Son (Jesus), God the Holy Spirit. The Holy Spirit is very real and alive. He speaks to us, but not in an audible way. He comes to us when we give our life to Christ, to lead us, guide us and helps us do more than we could do on our own. He receives the glory.

You will see clear evidence of God's activity through the book. Why, because He has our best interest at heart and He had mine.

The Holy Spirit reveals truth to you through scripture, a message when you need direction or a particular truth and He may even send someone in your life to minister to you.

Have you heard a sermon and felt as though it was spoken directly to you? That is the Holy Spirit trying to do a work in you. To discern that we are hearing Him speak to us, we need to know His word. We discover through His word how to live, our thoughts and controlling emotions, our actions and to be aware of His guidance.

"I waited patiently for the Lord; he turned to me and heard my cry." Psalm 40:1 (NIV)

When we pray and answers take longer than we expect, we need to be patient on hearing from God. If you have prayed about a situation and you lose interest, maybe God isn't speaking to you. If your prayer continues to increase and is in alignment with scripture, God has placed that desire on your heart. Be patient and wait for Him to speak to you.

"God I know the plans I have for you," says the Lord. "They are plans for good and not for disaster to give you a future and a hope." Jeremiah 29:11 (NLT)

He wants to walk and talk with us.

"My sheep listen to my voice; I know them, and they follow me. I give them eternal life, and they shall never perish, no one will snatch them out of my hand. My Father, who has given them to me, is greater than all, no one can snatch them out of the Father's hand and the Father are one." John 10: 27-30 (NIV)

When this book was placed on my heart it was in 2015. I knew I wanted to write this, but it just wasn't the right timing. In February of 2016, the desire to begin writing the stories was very strong. I would write as the Holy Spirit placed a story on my heart. As I was writing, I had researched the best time to publish a book and what that revealed was I had several months to complete this and take my time. After completing several chapters, the Holy Spirit led me to contact a pastor friend that is a professional author. I knew I could trust him to give me guidance with my book and the steps I needed to take for publishing. Due to a booked schedule, I was unable to meet with him. But, his secretary referred me to the publisher that his ministry uses and said they would be more than happy to speak with me. All God!

After contacting the publishing company that the ministry recommended, I found that the release date would be much sooner than I originally had planned. The Holy Spirit again was working. He knew that if I had taken several months to write this that maybe I would have been distracted and not completed the book. I had a tremendous desire and God knew that, so He had me where He wanted me to be and that was focused. Because I had already been working on the book, I prayed and made the decision to work diligently to meet the deadline. This would take most of my spare time, but worth getting the messages out. I feel that the readers will take something away from these that will comfort, encourage and inspire.

In order to meet the deadline, I was faced with difficult decisions. I had a beach trip planned with a friend and I knew if I went that I would not be focused on writing. There was pressure with that and even from my friend, to a point that made me feel guilty for choosing to stay home.

This was the conformation by the Holy Spirit that helped me realize I made the right decision. An e-mail from a friend, which read:

"Holding onto one thing always requires letting go of another. I'm sorry you missed the beach, but not sorry you chose a higher purpose. Congrats! The beach will be waiting for you when you are ready."

Another confirmation a friend shared, was something that she had seen on Fox News. A lady by the name of Jennifer Wilder Morgan had written a book similar to this and turned it into a screen play. She said "What in the world just happened? I'll tell you what happened. God happened. He opened doors and provided just the right people who would help me step through them."

Have you ever had a day when you really wanted to stay home, then something happened that made that possible? Now that you are home, you realize there was a purpose for that.

I have and when I did, I would watch Trinity Broadcasting Network for their inspirational and encouraging messages especially when I was walking through a challenging time. The messages would be exactly what I needed. Amen!

When times would hit and the enemy would place doubt I would receive the perfect words to press forward. Like this I received on one of those days.

> Friends may not always be present but the same God who spoke to Joshua is the same yesterday, today and forevermore." Be strong and of good courage, do not be afraid, nor be dismayed, for the Lord your God is with you wherever you go. Joshua 1:9

The one who stills the storms, walks on the waters, heals the sick, raises the dead, casts out demons is present with you wherever you are and what ever the time of day."

God's timing is perfect and He knows exactly what you need, just listen. He knows when to say "go" or "no" and hold you back. Do not rush an answer by jumping in and taking over.

"When you let go of what is in your hand, God will let go of what is in His hand," says Dr. Mike Murdock.

God is your source.

"Come to me, all you who are weary and burdened, and I will give you rest." Matthew 11:28 (NIV)

Unlock your future dream with God, sowing your seeds, where and who are you sowing for and the Lord will supply you with what you need. He wants you to be successful.

When in doubt I would read this, sent from a friend, over and over. "God does provide. That's the faith part. If God purposes something, He will provide what is necessary to make it reality. Faith and work go well together. Do your part. Lay the rest at His feet."

God was either placing friends in my life for encouraging words or I would hear a message that seemed to be spoken just for me. Why, because the desires of my dream to reach people through the stories would propel them forward.

When I was empty and didn't know what story to write. God would place the story, the title and words in my heart. He knew what was going to touch a life and He entrusted me with these.

Many are confused about the Holy Spirit and how He works.

- The Holy Spirit speaks in a still small quiet voice, a whisper. He does not yell or scream to get your attention.
- The Holy Spirit speaks through others. Maybe someone enters your life at just the right time and gives you the words you most needed to hear.
- The Holy Spirit speaks through written word, which is scripture, but sometimes may speak through our circumstances.

Sometimes we may miss the direction because we are living in disobedience. Living for self comes with consequences. You are taking your eyes off of God and ignoring His voice. There are times when God is trying to get your attention through trials that may come. The deeper you go with Him through your trials, the more you will learn to trust Him and the closer you will become.

You can walk alone and suffer through problems, which will play into Satan's hands or release the control and allow God to work. Knowing His word will help you move out of the way. Stand on His promises, He does not lie.

I know how weary and discouraging it is when you are trying to handle challenging times alone. I have cried out to God many times saying, "I can not do it anymore." That did not come as a shock to Him, He already knew that. He knows everything about us.

"For the Lord God is a sun and shield: the Lord will give grace and glory: no good thing will be withhold from them that walk uprightly." Psalm 84:11 (KJV)

If you don't have peace with an answer, don't do it. God is not one of confusion. Feeling pressure to make a decision is your "yellow flashing light" cautioning you to slow down and wait.

The Holy Spirit enjoys speaking to us when He may have our undivided attention. With me, it seems to be early mornings like 3:00 or 4:00 a.m. When your mind is filled with clutter, you will not be able to hear Him.

The tug on your heart or that gut feeling about something, is a way the Holy Spirit is leading you.

Being broken can be very painful, but that is when you release and submit yourself to God. We have many decisions and with those are choices. A choice to walk your own path or listen and follow God where there is hope in all you do.

My hope by sharing my experiences while writing this, along with the chapters of the book, you will see God at work.

About Tina Swann

Photo credit: Joseph De Sciose

In 1989, I joined the fitness industry as part time employment to earn income and this allowed me to set my hours around my two young daughters. Little did I know then, that this would become my full time profession. Working with the University of Alabama Huntsville (UAH), contracting with NASA and Huntsville Hospital as a Personal Trainer and Fitness Instructor. I also had the honor to train a young athlete in preparation for the 2004 Paralympic Volleyball Games in Athens, Greece. As I prepared this young lady to compete in these games, she was teaching me so much about life. I was her strength and conditioning coach, which certainly came with many different challenges yet she never gave up. Not just the physical pain that she would push through, but also the mindset to do so. She had faith even though she really didn't know what would lie ahead when arriving at the games. After training her, I began to look at Personal Training differently. Yes, it is guiding a person to be the best they can be. But also for them to see without a heart change and truly feeling this in their spirit, the mindset remains stagnate.

My heart began to change with clients that God would bring into my life. No longer were they just a client, but they were family. We were walking through the ups and downs of life together. Stories of God's Hand in Our Every Day Life.

And that is just it. God in our life. I have never been one that was good reciting scripture, but the scripture has lived in my heart. God's word would come to life in 2015. I never considered myself a writer when I felt the prompting to place the journaled stories into a book, but God had other plans. This was a step of faith for me and faith is not something hoped for, but an action. I would rely on God for strength because I am not an English major and this didn't come easily for me. One day when I was writing the fear that I can't was so overwhelming, so I stopped and called a friend. This is what she said, "Tina, write from your heart and the editing will come later." The voice of encouragement. Most have heard this:

"Can't Never Could Do Anything"

This is so true. As I mentioned the 'journaled' stories. God knew many years prior to 2015 that this book would be published and the stories brought to life so that you may know Him in a different way. He was aligning those needed to guide my path, like Dr. Jim Richards of Impact Ministries and World Changers. I have known Dr. Richards for many years and he is the author of great books such as Apocalypse, Moving Your Invisible Boundaries and How To Stop The Pain, to name just a few. So when I was looking for a publisher, his office connected me with Steve Spillman of True Potential Media. I have learned that writing is from my heart and becoming an author of this book is truly a step of faith. My faith is that these stories will reach many people that I may never personally meet and also places that I may never travel. May this book bring light into your life.

Thank you for reading *Followiing His Lead* and sharing this with others.

God Bless You, Tina Swann

www.ingramcontent.com/pod-product-compliance
Lightning Source LLC
LaVergne TN
LVHW051246080426
835513LV00016B/1767

* 9 7 8 1 9 4 8 7 9 4 4 0 4 *